The Mystical Meaning of **Hamlet**

Second Edition

Kenneth K. C. Chan

Quintessence of Dust: The Mystical Meaning of Hamlet

First Edition published in 2004
Second Edition 2024

ISBN
978-981-94-1041-5 (Paperback)
978-981-94-1043-9 (eBook)

National Library Board, Singapore Cataloguing in Publication Data

Name(s): Chan, Kenneth K. C.
Title: Quintessence of dust : the mystical meaning of Hamlet / Kenneth K. C. Chan.
Other Title(s): Mystical meaning of Hamlet
Description: Second edition. | Singapore : Kenneth K. C. Chan, 2024.
Identifier(s): ISBN 978-981-94-1041-5 (paperback) | 978-981-94-1043-9 (ebook)
Subject(s): LCSH: Shakespeare, William, 1564-1616--Criticism and interpretation.
| Hamlet (Legendary character)
Classification: DDC 822.33 --dc23

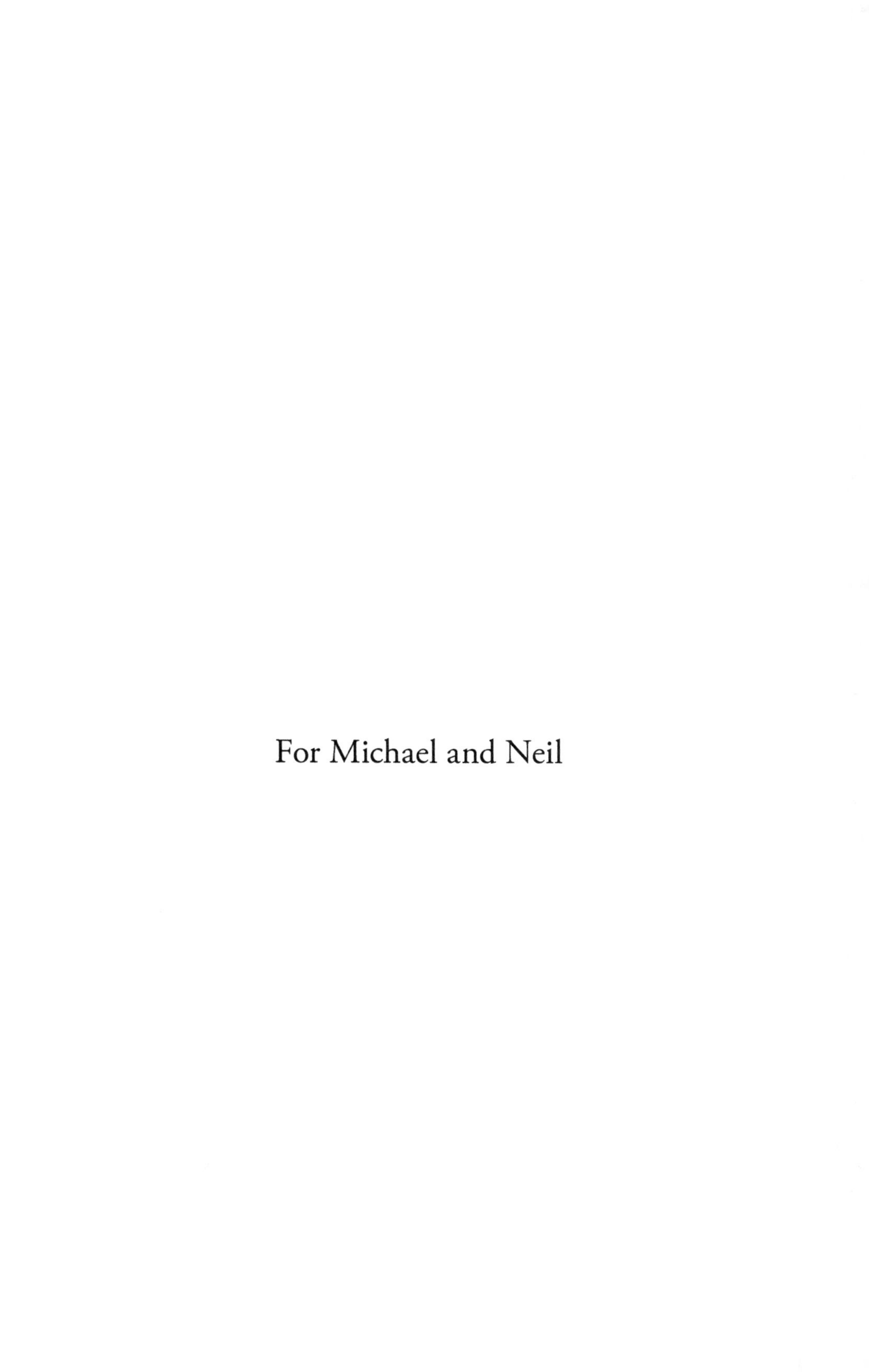

For Michael and Neil

Where there is hatred, let me sow love.
Where there is injury, pardon.

St Francis of Assisi

Other Books By The Same Author

The Mystical Art of Shakespeare Volume I: The Meaning of Much Ado About Nothing & The Comedy of Errors

The Mystical Art of Shakespeare Volume II: The Meaning of The Taming of the Shrew & Romeo and Juliet

Table of Contents

Acknowledgments

My heartfelt gratitude goes to all my inspirational guides in life, particularly to Lama Zopa Rinpoche, Penor Rinpoche, and Geshe Dorje Tashi.

Special thanks also to my editor, Debra Griffin, for improving the clarity and impact of the book.

The Mystical Art of Shakespeare

The transcendent light that burns within the text of a Shakespearean play is conveyed to us, in true mystical fashion, by absorbing our very being into the enactment of its meaning. The message of the play is not conveyed intellectually; it is experienced. The mystical art of Shakespeare is thus the art of initiation.

Shakespeare conveys his meaning by making us live through it. It is an emotional encounter designed to illuminate the universal spiritual principles within the depths of our own inner being. Shakespearean plays are thus akin to the mystery plays of old, where the initiate is introduced into the deeper mystical principles through the evocation of a heartfelt experience of their truth.

To truly imbibe the message of a Shakespearean play, we thus need to feel and breathe the life of the drama as though it were real. We must plunge ourselves fully into the action and live through the performance. This is the experience of a true mystical theatre. It is learning through emotional participation, an encounter that always leaves a deeper impression than mere textbook learning. This initiatic quality is the very nature of the esoteric art of Shakespeare.

Shakespeare crafts every play meticulously to make us experience the truth of its message. This is clearly evident because of three distinctive traits, found in all Shakespearean plays, that reveal this nature of the playwright's intent:

1. Cohesive Unity

The meaning of a Shakespearean play resides in the experience of the play as a cohesive whole. While it is well recognized that a good short essay should be unified, Shakespeare extends this principle of unity to the entire play, so much so that there are no extraneous scenes in a Shakespearean play. Each play constitutes a tightly bound unit, carefully crafted to leave its impact as a single compact entity. We may call this characteristic quality—found in every Shakespearean play—a "cohesive unity" of meaning, since every part of the play contributes towards the central theme.

It is thus improper to base our interpretation of any Shakespearean play on a mere selected portion of the play, in a way that renders the rest of the same play irrelevant (or even contradictory to our interpretation). If we extract a portion of a Shakespearean play, we can almost certainly interpret this isolated segment in diverse ways. Some critics then claim it impossible to determine clear authorial intent. This is a fallacy because it ignores the cohesive unity in all Shakespearean plays.

Different interpretations are possible only if we consider bits of the play separately in isolation. Diversity in interpretation is virtually impossible if we interpret the entire play as a cohesive whole. Shakespeare's intent will then be clear. The meaning of a Shakespearean play lies in the experience of it as a single coherent entity, and any interpretation must heed this unity of purpose.

To make the play function as a cohesive whole, Shakespeare's opening scene introduces the play's main area of concern. The subsequent few scenes then elaborate on this area of concern and bring the central theme into focus. Shakespeare then keeps our focus on this central theme through the second characteristic technique found in all his plays.

2. Thematic Resonance

As each Shakespearean play imparts its message through our emotional experience, the central meaning is repeated many times throughout the play. The dominant themes of the play reverberate through the entire drama, like a long rolling thunder that often builds, from the beginning, to a resounding climax at the end. We may call this unique trait of ever-repeating motifs in Shakespeare's plays "thematic resonance"—a technique of flooding our subconscious with an incessant flow of recurring impressions that convey the deeper meaning to our inner being.

While it may be difficult, at times, to discern accurately the intent of other authors through their narrative writings, the thematic resonance

found in Shakespeare's works makes his intent patently clear. We should look for the meaning of a Shakespearean play in the motifs that echo incessantly from start to finish. It is this characteristic in Shakespeare's plays that makes it so evident what Shakespeare's intended meaning is.

In this sense, Shakespeare's plays stand out uniquely from other literary works. By employing thematic resonance, Shakespeare is able—despite the instability of meaning in language—to provide stability to the meaning of his plays. In other words, he drives home his message by relentlessly repeating it.

3. Focused Allegorical Scenes

Another vital clue to the meaning of a Shakespearean play resides in scenes that do not directly contribute to the main action. There are often many scenes in a Shakespearean play that appear unnecessary to the plot and which may even be considered mere comic relief. Nonetheless, they are there for a specific reason for they contribute to the play's central meaning.

We shall call all these apparently extraneous scenes "focused allegorical scenes" because they artistically amplify the main themes of the play using symbolism, analogy or parody. These allegorical scenes can be called "focused" because they all contribute towards advancing the central message. It is this unified focus of all the allegorical scenes in any one play that makes this evidence of authorial intent so compelling. These scenes now provide us with some of the best clues to Shakespeare's intended meaning.

While allegorical scenes, taken in isolation, may be interpreted in diverse ways, these same allegorical scenes, taken in combination with the cohesive unity and thematic resonance in the play, become clear in their intended meaning. These focused allegorical scenes are designed to artistically amplify the themes already suggested by Shakespeare in the main action of the play.

* * *

If we heed the three characteristic traits found in all Shakespearean plays—their cohesive unity, thematic resonance, and focused allegorical scenes—the intended meaning of each play is patently clear. These distinctive traits must be seriously considered because they cannot exist unless Shakespeare meticulously crafted them. Something so consistent and elaborate cannot occur by chance. It would be a travesty to persist in interpreting Shakespeare's plays while ignoring what he deliberately crafts into them.

While the meaning of each play is obvious from its cohesive unity, thematic resonance, and focused allegorical scenes, there is yet another clue to the meaning of Shakespeare's plays if we consider them collectively. Shakespeare wrote his plays all with the intent of conveying deep spiritual principles. Thus his collection of plays actually forms a cohesive whole. Each play focuses on a different aspect of the spiritual path, and they all complement one other. An awareness of this fact is another useful tool in understanding each play.

In the following pages, we will find the above traits manifesting through the entire play of Shakespeare's *Hamlet*. As these traits are also evident in all of Shakespeare's plays, an intriguing question arises: If all Shakespearean plays characteristically demonstrate these qualities in their construction—qualities that render clearly the meaning of his plays—why then has this meaning eluded critics for centuries?

The answer resides in the unique spiritual nature of the messages behind Shakespeare's plays. Shakespeare's messages target the average person, unlike those found in most other literary works that, instead, target those considered "below average" in morality. The messages of these other literary works are generally not applicable to the average majority, since the majority has no need for them, and this ironically allows the average person to accept their meaning readily. Since these messages do not require a change in one's perspective on life, there is no problem accepting them.

Shakespeare's messages, however, uniquely target the average person, which means you and I. Shakespeare's messages directly apply to us, and may involve principles we do not yet fully understand. A full acceptance of Shakespeare's meaning may require a change in our perspective on life or even our lifestyle, and change generates resistance. Consciously or subconsciously, we may choose to avoid hearing the message. That is probably the reason why the meaning behind a Shakespearean play is often missed: We miss it because we do not want to hear it.

Yet, it is for this very reason that Shakespeare's plays are of such importance. His messages target us because we need to hear them.

Shakespeare's plays thus constitute a timeless and invaluable gift to humanity, a living legacy that conveys a deep spiritual meaning we particularly need to appreciate at this critical time of human history.

It is because Shakespeare's plays are invested with such profound meaning that they often have an enthralling—and almost hypnotic—grip upon our subconscious. The plays have this lyrical mesmerizing quality because they touch something deep within us, like a reminder of something profound we may have long forgotten yet resides within the inner recesses of our being.

It is important that we also try to understand, beyond the subconscious level, the messages behind Shakespeare's plays; for they are the same universal messages that past sages have long tried to impart to a suffering humanity. A deeper understanding of Shakespeare's meaning will enhance the experiential initiatic quality of his plays, and help evoke the actual experience of living through the mystical principles they convey. Shakespeare's plays thus constitute an invaluable tool that we may use to help us along the long road towards true mystical illumination of the deeper spiritual principles of the universe.

How to Read Shakespeare

All of Shakespeare's plays are meticulously crafted to deliver deep spiritual messages, and these messages are conveyed through our emotional involvement in the drama. The meaning of each play is found in what the whole action of the play moves us to feel. Here lies the true art of Shakespeare. He reaches us by emotionally absorbing us in the play's message. Thus, the message in each play takes the form of an emotional appeal that is conveyed to our right brain, our sensitive, emotional and intuitive mind. And here, all the poetry and imagery becomes vital. Here, the incredible artistry of Shakespeare becomes a living legacy.

An understanding of how Shakespeare imparts his meaning also leads us to the correct approach to his plays. We need to immerse ourselves in the action as though it were truly happening. We should not over-interpret the words of the characters, looking for hidden nuances between the lines. We should not interpret the characters as representing something else not openly presented by Shakespeare. Instead, we need to accept the action of the play as though it were real, because the meaning is conveyed through our emotional participation.

When Hamlet accidentally kills Polonius, we are to take it that Hamlet accidentally kills Polonius, and not, for instance, that it depicts our spiritual nature (represented by Hamlet) destroying our rationalizing mind (represented by Polonius). Or as the reformist movement (Hamlet) striking against the orthodox church (Polonius), or anything of that kind. This type of over-interpretation destroys the aim of the play, which is to immerse us emotionally in its message. We no longer feel the tragedy and horror of the action if we interpret it as a mere symbolical representation of something else. The art and poetry are then rendered useless, and a standard textbook will convey the message just as effectively.

At times, the action in Shakespeare's plays is partly allegorical or symbolic, as in a focused allegorical scene. In such instances, however, the allegory or symbolism is related to what is already portrayed in the drama and serves as an artistic means to amplify its impact. We must not interpret the play as an allegory of something that Shakespeare does not suggest directly. If we do that, we may miss the message entirely.

We should also not look for the meaning in hidden nuances between the lines of the characters. Shakespeare portrays all his points very dramatically. Also, the message lies in the direct impact of the drama in its entirety and is seldom encapsulated in any one or two lines of the characters. Much less is it to be found in hidden subtleties not openly portrayed. For instance, when Hamlet pours verbal abuse on Ophelia in Act III, Scene 1, we are not to read between the lines that Hamlet is doing so because he realizes that Polonius is hidden behind the arras, listening in. If that were the case, Shakespeare would make it obvious. Once again, we should take what is presented to us as it appears. Otherwise, we will miss the emotional impact as Shakespeare intends.

Also, the words spoken by the characters are always true to their character. They say what their personalities will say, not necessarily what Shakespeare himself feels about the topic. This is what makes the drama so realistic. Thus, the meaning of the plays need not be found in any particular words spoken by the players. The meaning comes from the whole drama and resides in the emotional experience of the entire play.

Thus, when we read Shakespeare—instead of watching the play—we must do so with emotional involvement, picturing the scene laid before us as real. We need to use our imagination to fill in the dramatic visuals and sounds of the scene. For it is only by immersing ourselves in the play, making each scene live in us as though it were real, that the true message will reach us. Then we will learn through the experience, and it becomes a part of our psyche. This is a far more valuable lesson than any intellectual teaching can achieve.

It is thus helpful to read a play in two ways. One reading should be as a form of critical study to understand the artistic techniques that Shakespeare employs to impart his message. The other reading, on a separate occasion, should be in the nature of an emotional involvement. Here, we immerse ourselves and live through the play as though it were real. This second reading is essential to truly gain the message. We learn because in a sense, we live through it, and it becomes a part of us. The emotional reading is like an initiation. And it is here that the artistry of Shakespeare truly comes alive.

Prologue: *The Mystery of Hamlet*

There are two mysteries in *Hamlet*, the mystery of the meaning of the play as Shakespeare intends, and the larger mystery—the ultimate mystery of life—that the play addresses. Let us look, here, at the first mystery: What is Shakespeare trying to say in *Hamlet*?

This question so perplexed critics over the last four hundred years that many finally concluded, after immense struggle, that there is no central message in *Hamlet*. The play seems to lack a cohesive theme and remains an enigma. It appears that Shakespeare merely created an astonishing piece of art that haunts us continually but lacks a binding philosophy. Nothing, in fact, is more wrong.

Part of the central message in *Hamlet* is so dramatically portrayed by Shakespeare that it is almost sublime. I refer to Act III, Scene 4, which virtually sets this theme on fire. The scene is also a source of dismay to the audience because Hamlet displays a callous lack of remorse after accidentally killing Polonius, the elderly Councilor of State. Hamlet even proceeds to ridicule the slain man:

Hamlet I'll lug the guts into the neighbour room.
Mother, good night indeed. This counsellor
Is now most still, most secret, and most grave,
Who was in life a foolish prating knave.

Someone who can react in this way hardly fits the image of an ideal hero. Surely Polonius deserves some measure of compassion. Why then does Shakespeare not spare Hamlet even a single word of kindness for Polonius? This would have greatly helped to redeem his hero and would have been simple for Shakespeare to implement. Shakespeare, instead, does the opposite. The next three scenes continue with Hamlet's bizarre and disgusting antics over the body of Polonius, as though Shakespeare wants to assure us Hamlet's lack of remorse is no oversight. It is deliberate. Why?

Let us return to Act III, Scene 4, and picture the drama. The scene opens with Polonius indulging in his petty court intrigues by concealing himself behind the curtains to spy on the coming encounter between Hamlet and his mother. Hamlet arrives, having already worked himself into a fearsome state of mind. We know his state of mind from the two preceding scenes. At the end of Act III, Scene 2, after confirming for himself that his uncle—the current king—had indeed murdered his father, as the ghost informs, Hamlet says:

Hamlet 'Tis now the very witching time of night,
When churchyards yawn and hell itself breathes out
Contagion to this world. Now could I drink hot blood,
And do such bitter business as the day
Would quake to look on.

Hamlet thus prepares himself for revenge. So wild has he become that even the thought of killing his mother enters his mind, but he suppresses it:

Hamlet Oh heart, lose not thy nature. Let not ever
The soul of Nero[1] enter this firm bosom;
Let me be cruel, not unnatural.
I will speak daggers to her, but use none.

His state worsens in the next scene (Act III, Scene 3) when he stumbles on the King praying. He rejects this opportunity to kill the King because the act of praying may help redeem him. Hamlet's motive for revenge has gone beyond merely the establishment of justice in this world. It is a darker motive of pure malice; he decides to postpone his revenge to a more "opportune" moment, so that he can unleash an eternity of suffering upon his victim:

Hamlet Up sword, and know thou a more horrid hent:[2]
When he is drunk asleep, or in his rage,
Or in th'incestuous pleasure of his bed,
At game a-swearing, or about some act
That has no relish[3] of salvation in't,
Then trip him that his heels may kick at heaven
And that his soul may be as damned and black
As hell, whereto it goes.

---

1 **Nero** Roman emperor who had his mother murdered

2 **hent** occasion, opportunity

3 **relish** trace

Thus, in this fearsome and malevolent state of mind, Hamlet now appears before his mother in Act III, Scene 4. His mother quickly perceives his mood after a short exchange of words and tries to end the meeting by leaving. Hamlet prevents her, causing her to cry for help. Polonius, behind the curtains, echoes her cry, and Hamlet summarily kills him by thrusting his sword through the arras, thinking he is the King. Now the real dramatic point begins.

Picture the scene. Polonius lies dead on the stage, newly slain by Hamlet. The Queen cries:

Queen Oh what a rash and bloody deed is this!

What is Hamlet's response?

Hamlet A bloody deed. Almost as bad, good mother,
As kill a king and marry with his brother.

This response is a study of Hamlet's mind in a nutshell. His initial reaction spares no compassionate thought over the death of Polonius. He is fixated on condemning his mother and his uncle.

Hamlet then appeals passionately to his mother to realize the error of her hasty remarriage. The anguished Queen eventually cries out for Hamlet to stop.

Queen Oh Hamlet, speak no more.
Thou turn'st my eyes into my very soul,
And there I see such black and grained[4] spots
As will not leave their tinct.[5]

Yet Hamlet, in his passion, does not let go:

Hamlet Nay, but to live
In the rank sweat of an enseamed[6] bed,
Stewed in corruption, honeying and making love
Over the nasty sty!

The Queen makes another anguished appeal:

4 **grained** fast-dyed, indelible

5 **tinct** color

6 **enseamed** greasy

Queen Oh speak to me no more.
These words like daggers enter in my ears.
No more, sweet Hamlet.

Yet Hamlet persists:

Hamlet A murderer and a villain,
A slave that is not twentieth part the tithe[7]
Of your precedent lord, a vice[8] of kings,
A cutpurse of the empire and the rule,
That from a shelf the precious diadem stole
And put it in his pocket—

All this is almost commendable, a measure of Hamlet's intense mourning for his lost father, except for one glaring fact: The body of Polonius is lying on the stage in full view of the audience.

Now the ghost of Hamlet's father enters, and Hamlet expresses his guilt at having delayed the revenge he promised.

Hamlet Do you not come your tardy son to chide
That, lapsed in time and passion, lets go by
Th'important acting of your dread command?
Oh say.

Again, Hamlet's expression of a deep filial bond with his late father is almost commendable—but the body of Polonius still lies in full view. This almost unbelievable scene reveals Shakespeare at his most sublime. What is Shakespeare trying to say?

We witness an impassioned, almost moral, appeal by Hamlet to his mother to realize the error of her hasty remarriage while he blatantly contravenes all sense of compassion to a fellow being, newly slain by his own hand. We also witness his filial guilt for the delay in avenging his father while he totally neglects and even mocks the death of another. When the ghost of Hamlet's father arrives to remind him of his "almost blunted purpose," we may wonder why the ghost of Polonius does not get up and reprimand the other ghost.

---

7 **tithe** tenth part

8 **vice** a character (often the buffoon) in morality plays

The whole episode is surreal, its dramatic impact nearly unbelievable. There is no doubt that Shakespeare deliberately set it up, for he neatly places the entire episode between two striking passages of Hamlet mocking the slain man. What is his purpose?

It is, in fact, a message of great profundity, a deeply spiritual one that touches on the ultimate mystery of life, and one not easy to come to terms with. So Shakespeare does not blatantly state it in written words. Instead, he crafts the entire play into an emotional and passionate appeal to the audience to see its truth. The result is an astounding piece of art. For *Hamlet* is one of the greatest pieces of literature we possess, great both in its poetic artistry and in its deep meaning.

Let us now begin a closer exploration of its mystery.

1

Act I

Scene 1

The opening scene in a Shakespearean play usually introduces the area of concern that the play addresses. In *Hamlet*, the opening scene dramatically evokes the mystery world we are all in, the thinly veiled situation of every man, caught between the mundane world of the senses and the wider spiritual world just a shade beyond. We are treading on a divide, stranded on a wall separating the seen and the vast unseen. On the bleak battlements of a cold windswept night, the setting of the opening scene, we may be keenly aware of the divide. This mystery world is the play's area of concern.

The exposition in Shakespeare's plays also sets the tone and mood of the play. In *Hamlet*, it evokes an aura of mystery and a confrontation with the unknown. From the beginning, this sense of suspense and underlying mystery pervades the entire play.

The action begins at midnight, on the stark platform of the castle wall.

Barnardo Who's there?

Francisco Nay, answer me. Stand and unfold[1] yourself.

Barnardo Long live the King!

Francisco Barnardo?

Barnardo He.

Significantly, Barnardo, the relieving guard, wrongly issues the first challenge, suggesting an atmosphere of mistrust.

---

1 **unfold** identify

Francisco	You come most carefully upon your hour.
Barnardo	'Tis now struck twelve. Get thee to bed, Francisco.
Francisco	For this relief, much thanks. 'Tis bitter cold, And I am sick at heart.

In a few lines, Shakespeare brilliantly establishes the tone of uncertainty and apprehension, and he maintains this tone throughout the play.

Barnardo	Have you had quiet guard?
Francisco	Not a mouse stirring.
Barnardo	Well, good night. If you do meet Horatio and Marcellus, The rivals[2] of my watch, bid them make haste.
Francisco	I think I hear them.

Soon, Horatio and Marcellus arrive at the battlements. Francisco exits, leaving Barnardo at the watch.

Marcellus	Holla, Barnardo!
Barnardo	Say, what, is Horatio there?
Horatio	A piece of him.

Horatio means that he is here only half willingly. We soon find out why, and the sense of premonition deepens when we learn of the appearance of an apparition, a contact with the beyond.

Barnardo	Welcome, Horatio. Welcome, good Marcellus.
Horatio	What, has this thing appeared again tonight?
Barnardo	I have seen nothing.
Marcellus	Horatio says 'tis but our fantasy, And will not let belief take hold of him, Touching this dreaded sight twice seen of us. Therefore I have entreated him along

2 **rivals** partners

With us to watch the minutes of this night,
That if again this apparition come,
He may approve[3] our eyes and speak to it.

Horatio Tush, tush, 'twill not appear.

Horatio's response on being told of the apparition is typical of many when confronted with suggestions of the beyond. He dismisses it as impossible. Yet he is here to see the apparition for himself if it does appear.

To fully appreciate the play, we should place ourselves in the same situation and open our minds to the possibilities of the unknown, the world beyond the mundane one limited by our sensory perception and our scientific apparatus. We must realize that it is presumptuous to assume that our senses and our machines can detect everything.

Barnardo Sit down awhile,
And let us once again assail your ears,
That are so fortified against our story,
What we two nights have seen.

Horatio Well, sit we down.
And let us hear Barnardo speak of this.

Barnardo Last night of all,
When yond same star that's westward from the pole,[4]
Had made his course t'illume that part of heaven
Where now it burns, Marcellus and myself,
The bell then beating one—

Now, the actual apparition suddenly appears.

Marcellus Peace, break thee off. Look where it comes again.

Barnardo In the same figure like the King that's dead.

Marcellus Thou art a scholar. Speak to it, Horatio.

Barnardo Looks it not like the King? Mark it, Horatio.

Horatio Most like. It harrows me with fear and wonder.

---

3 **approve** corroborate

4 **pole** Pole star

On the urging of Barnardo and Marcellus, Horatio questions the apparition.

Horatio What art thou that usurp'st this time of night,
Together with that fair and warlike form
To which the majesty of buried Denmark[5]
Did sometimes march? By heaven, I charge thee speak.

Marcellus It is offended.

Barnardo See, it stalks away.

Horatio Stay, speak, speak, I charge thee speak!

The nature of the ghost is important in the play. Horatio questions its identity, an issue that also concerns Hamlet later. More crucial to the theme of the play, however, is whether the ghost holds any moral or spiritual authority. This is made clear subsequently.

After the ghost's appearance, the guards ask Horatio the reason for the war preparations; his answer introduces the first of the four parallel actions in the play. The former king of Norway, Fortinbras, had been killed by Hamlet's father in single matched combat, and had also forfeited lands to the conqueror under the terms of a formal agreement. Now his son is the first character in the play who seeks to avenge a father's death.

Horatio Now sir, young Fortinbras,
Of unimproved[6] mettle, hot and full,
Hath in the skirts[7] of Norway here and there
Sharked up[8] a list of lawless resolutes
For food and diet to some enterprise
That hath a stomach in't;[9] which is no other,
As it doth well appear unto our state,
But to recover of us by strong hand
And terms compulsatory those foresaid lands
So by his father lost.

---

5 **buried Denmark** the buried King of Denmark

6 **unimproved** undisciplined

7 **skirts** borders

8 **sharked up** gathered up indiscriminately

9 **hath a stomach in't** requires courage

Three more characters face the same situation of having a father killed: Hamlet himself, Laertes, and Pyrrhus (portrayed in a speech by Hamlet and one of the traveling players). Parallel action is one of the main methods employed in Renaissance drama to project a theme and its meaning through contrast and analogy. It enriches and generalizes the issue in question. In *Hamlet*, we have four parallel actions on one theme—the theme of revenge.

The talk of war and the preparations for it deepen the sense of apprehension in this opening scene. Horatio adds to it further with allusions of other portents and omens:

Horatio A mote it is to trouble the mind's eye.
In the most high and palmy state of Rome,
A little ere the mightiest Julius fell,
The graves stood tenantless and the sheeted dead
Did squeak and gibber in the Roman streets;
As stars with trains of fire and dews of blood,
Disasters [10] in the sun; and the moist star, [11]
Upon whose influence Neptune's empire stands, [12]
Was sick almost to doomsday with eclipse.

This passage is a reference by Shakespeare to his other play, *Julius Caesar*, which appeared close to the time of *Hamlet*. He mentions Julius Caesar again in Act III, Scene 2, in the dialogue between Hamlet and Polonius, and yet again in Act V, Scene 1, at the graveyard scene. Shakespeare has a reason for reminding us of this other play, for the message in *Julius Caesar*, dramatically depicted in the nature of the storm, also appears as an issue in *Hamlet*. Let us digress briefly for a closer look at the crucial message in *Julius Caesar*.

One of the main protagonists in *Julius Caesar* is Brutus. He is the dramatic hero of the play, portrayed as noble throughout. His admirable qualities are summed up at the end of the play:

---

10 **disasters** ominous signs

11 **moist star** moon

12 **Neptune's empire stands** the seas depend

Antony This was the noblest Roman of them all.
All the conspirators save only he
Did that they did in envy of great Caesar;
He only, in a general honest thought
And common good to all, made one of them.[13]
His life was gentle,[14] and the elements
So mix'd in him, that Nature might stand up
And say to all the world, 'This was a man!'

Yet Brutus, with his noble mind and honest motives, still makes the fatal error of collaborating in the assassination of Caesar. How does he go wrong, and where is his error? In the answer lies the central message of the play, and, characteristically, Shakespeare does not state it blatantly. Instead, he portrays it in a way that leaves a lasting vivid impression.

The dramatic image in *Julius Caesar* comes in the form of the fearsome storm, replete with supernatural omens, the night before Caesar's assassination. It rages through three scenes of the play and the players graphically describe it:

Casca Are you not mov'd, when all the sway of earth
Shakes like a thing unfirm? O, Cicero,
I have seen tempests, when the scolding winds
Have rived[15] the knotty oaks; and I have seen
The ambitious ocean swell and rage and foam,
To be exalted with[16] the threat'ning clouds:
But never till tonight, never till now,
Did I go through a tempest dropping fire.
Either there is civil strife in heaven,
Or else the world, too saucy with the gods,
Incenses them to send destruction.

In such a storm, we can only watch the raging elements in helpless awe and feel the presence of the transcendent beyond in the universal

---

13 **made one of them** joined the conspirators

14 **gentle** noble

15 **rived** split

16 **exalted with** elevated to

vastness and power. Yet Brutus ignores it; instead, he agonizes in a purely intellectual debate on his course of action when, in the dark of night, he struggles to read from a piece of paper deviously planted by Cassius to influence his decision:

Brutus The exhalations[17] whizzing in the air
Give so much light that I may read by them.

Brutus ignores the meteors and the raging heavens, and ironically uses the light from the sky to focus instead on intellectually working out his course of action. This is the dramatic image of his error. He ignores the spiritual and the mystical and does not align himself with the divine laws of the universe. We may say, in the manner of Lao Tzu, that he heeds not the Tao and does not flow with it. The divine influence in his being is missing in his decision-making. In a matter of such moral significance as murder, it is a tragic error. Keep this in mind, for a similar theme occurs in *Hamlet*.

We return now to the opening scene in *Hamlet*, where amid the bleak battlements of the castle wall, Horatio tells us that similar omens have appeared in Denmark.

Horatio And even the like precurse[18] of feared events,
As harbingers[19] preceding still the fates
And prologue to the omen[20] coming on,
Have heaven and earth together demonstrated
Unto our climatures and countrymen.

Now the ghost reappears, and Horatio again attempts to learn from it.

Horatio Stay, illusion:
If thou hast any sound or use of voice,
Speak to me.
If there be any good thing to be done

---

17 **exhalations** meteors

18 **precurse** advance warning

19 **harbingers** forerunners

20 **omen** calamity portended

That may to thee do ease, and grace to me,
Speak to me;
If thou art privy to thy country's fate,
Which, happily, foreknowing may avoid,
Oh speak;
Or if thou hast uphoarded in thy life
Extorted treasure in the womb of earth,
For which, they say, you spirits oft walk in death,
Speak of it. Stay and speak! [*The cock crows*]
Stop it, Marcellus.

Horatio prefaces each question with a condition that the answer be beneficial. He is unsure, as we should also be, whether any counsel from the ghost will be sound or ill advised. What happens next suggests that we should indeed be wary of the ghost's words. At the crowing of the cock, it leaves hurriedly without speaking; Horatio explains:

Horatio And then it started like a guilty thing
Upon a fearful summons. I have heard
The cock, that is the trumpet to the morn,
Doth with his lofty and shrill-sounding throat
Awake the god of day, and at his warning,
Whether in sea or fire, in earth or air,
Th'extravagant and erring[21] spirit hies
To his confine; and of the truth herein
This present object made probation.[22]

There should be little doubt, then, that the ghost is no angel, and his advice must also be suspect. Shakespeare stresses this crucial point here and again in Scenes 2 and 5. Marcellus now reinforces the point:

Marcellus It faded on the crowing of the cock.
Some say that ever 'gainst[23] that season comes
Wherein our Saviour's birth is celebrated,
The bird of dawning singeth all night long;

21 **extravagant and erring** wandering out of bounds

22 **probation** proof

23 **'gainst** just before

And then, they say, no spirit dare stir abroad,
The nights are wholesome; then no planets strike,[24]
No fairy takes,[25] nor witch hath power to charm,
So hallowed and so gracious is that time.

Horatio So have I heard and do in part believe it.
But look, the morn in russet[26] mantle clad
Walks o'er the dew of yon high eastern hill.
Break we our watch up, and by my advice
Let us impart what we have seen tonight
Unto young Hamlet; for upon my life
This spirit, dumb to us, will speak to him.

Dawn breaks and the opening scene ends with the three men resolving to recount their night's experience to Hamlet. We have witnessed an evocation of man's spiritual state, a state of being stranded on a divide between the mundane world and the great beyond. On the stark platform of a castle wall on a cold bleak night, we have experienced a confrontation with the profound, a confrontation with the ultimate mystery—the mystery of death and the beyond. This mystical world on the narrow divide between the mundane and the spiritual, combined with the issue of confronting the profound, is the play's central concern.

The next scene presents another encounter with the profound, that concerning death, an encounter from which, in real life, we cannot hope to escape.

---

24 **strike** exert evil influence

25 **takes** bewitches

26 **russet** coarse reddish-brown cloth

Scene 2

Part of the artistry in Shakespeare's plays lies in the placement of the scenes and the way one scene influences the emotional impact of the next. This effect is important now as we shift from the bleak battlements of the castle wall to the royal court of Denmark, where, in the presence of Hamlet, the King and Queen are at council. While the ghost of Hamlet's father lingers in our minds, we witness his brother's response to his death.

King Though yet of Hamlet our dear brother's death
The memory be green; and that it us befitted
To bear our hearts in grief, and our whole kingdom
To be contracted in one brow of woe;
Yet so far hath discretion fought with nature
That we with wisest sorrow think on him,
Together with remembrance of ourselves.
Therefore our[27] sometime sister,[28] now our queen,
Th'imperial jointress[29] of this warlike state,
Have we, as 'twere with a defeated joy,
With an auspicious and a dropping eye,
With mirth in funeral and with dirge in marriage,
In equal scale weighing delight and dole,
Taken to wife.

Thus we learn that Hamlet's uncle has married his recently widowed mother and is now the king of Denmark. Knowing that the ghost of Hamlet's father is still stalking the battlements at night, we feel the uncle's lack of sincere sorrow, and its effect is certainly not lost on Hamlet.

The King next turns his attention to the threat of Fortinbras who has demanded the surrender of the lands his father had lost to the former king of Denmark. We learn that Fortinbras's uncle, the King of Norway, being bedridden, is apparently unaware of Fortinbras's activities. In an attempt to restrain Fortinbras, the King now dispatches Cornelius and Voltemand as envoys to alert the King of Norway to his nephew's plans.

---

27 **our** the royal "we"

28 **sometime sister** former sister-in-law

29 **jointress** partner

The King then greets Laertes, the son of Polonius, the elderly Councilor of State. Laertes requests the King's permission to return to France, and this is granted on the agreement of Polonius.

Finally, the King speaks to Hamlet:

King But now, my cousin Hamlet, and my son—

Hamlet A little more than kin, and less than kind.

Hamlet's famous opening line immediately reveals his resentment at the incestuous relationship between his uncle and his mother. It also reveals a very noticeable facet of Hamlet's character—his ability to unleash sharp witty comments even in the depths of despair.

We can interpret Hamlet's first remark in a number of ways. "A little more than kin" probably refers to the unnatural way by which Hamlet has become the son of his uncle while "less than kind" may refer both to the difference Hamlet perceives between himself and his uncle and to the lack of kindliness in his uncle, particularly in his hurried marriage to his mother. Full of double meanings and innuendoes, Hamlet's lines have intrigued literary critics for centuries.

King How is it that the clouds still hang on you?

Hamlet Not so, my lord, I am too much i'th'sun.

Hamlet's response reverberates with double meanings. Is his sorrow insufficient to meet the circumstances? Or, considering the pun between the words "sun" and "son," is he too much of a true son not to be in a state of grief? Or is it "too much" that he is now the son of his uncle? Hamlet's bitterness continually manifests itself in his sharp wit. Now the Queen pleads with him:

Queen Good Hamlet, cast thy nighted colour off,
And let thine eye look like a friend on Denmark.
Do not for ever with thy vailed[30] lids
Seek for thy noble father in the dust.
Thou know'st 'tis common: all that lives must die,
Passing through nature to eternity.

Hamlet Ay, madam, it is common.

---

[30] **vailed** downcast

Queen If it be,
Why seems it so particular with thee?

This question brings up a crucial point in the play. What the Queen and, later, the King suggests is that since death is common, we should not be too concerned about it. But such an attitude is totally illogical. Not only is death common, it is also inevitable. And if death is inevitable, it follows that we should indeed be very concerned about it.

Here is our first encounter with the question that Shakespeare poses for us repeatedly throughout the play: How do we respond to this inevitability of death? Do we simply do nothing other than distract ourselves from the truth with futile and petty actions? Unfortunately, distraction is the common response, our usual method of coping with death, which is to say, we do not cope at all; we hide from reality.

This tendency of ours to hide from the profound is exactly what Shakespeare wants to focus our attention on. Why? What is his purpose? To answer this question, we need to realize that Shakespeare is actually a highly advanced being, a person with a profound understanding of the spiritual path. We find evidence of his spiritual nature in the deep spiritual messages he conveys to us in all his plays. [31]

In *Hamlet*, Shakespeare is trying to get us to ask this question: Might there not be a better way of responding to the inevitability of death other than hiding from the truth? Might we not, instead, take heed of the words of Plato when he says: "Of some things I am not sure, but I am sure of one thing: that it is better and more manly to think that we ought to investigate what we do not know than idly assume that we cannot, or ought not to, investigate. For this I would fight to the limit of my power in word and deed."

Indeed, how do we know there is no solution unless we investigate? Might we not find the courage to venture into the heart of the ultimate

---

[31] These messages provide evidence for Shakespeare's spiritual nature because they are not derived from a mere intellectual interpretation of any particular religion's scriptural doctrine. The nature of the messages strongly suggests that they are the direct realizations of an advanced mystic who has actually undertaken the arduous task of transforming his life and personality towards the spiritual ideal. True aspirants of the spiritual path—the saints and the bodhisattvas—attain their realizations from direct experience.

mystery? Why do we meekly succumb to despair without even taking a single step and proceed to bury ourselves in the petty distractions of the mundane? Will not the futile attempt to hide from the inevitable merely enhance the fearful certainty? What do we have to lose by trying to penetrate the veil?

Attempting to penetrate the veil essentially means taking the spiritual path. This in no way means surrendering ourselves to a blind faith. Blind faith in dogma is not a solution, since we may end up believing in something that is incorrect. The true spiritual path is a path of verification. We find our way through a process of knowing, a process of verifying the truths as they unfold before us.

Shakespeare knows that all of us have within us an inner light that will illuminate the darkness. We must find this inner light; it will allow us to experience the truths for ourselves and find a passage through the darkness. We will know because we will experience the truths directly. There is, however, only one way to verify that this process works—we have to make the journey ourselves.

This, in the end, is what Shakespeare wants us to do. But first, we must find the courage to face the inevitability of death, to admit to the truth, and to confront the profound. For only by doing so will we discover the powerful motivation to embark on the spiritual quest, and only then will we have the deep strength to transform our lives in accordance with the truth.

That is why, in *Hamlet*, Shakespeare creates a thematic resonance that repeatedly places this question before us: Are we able to accept the inevitability of death and confront the profound? To emphasize the importance of this question, practically all the main characters in the play eventually die. All of them, like us, must ultimately face the profound whether or not we prepare ourselves for it.

How each of the characters avoids confronting the inevitability of death is dramatically portrayed in the play, providing a picture of the whole spectrum of man's varied reactions to the truth of our mortality. Their behavior thus represents the wide range of distractions we employ in our futile attempts to hide from the inevitable.

Among the characters in the play, Hamlet is the only one courageous enough to confront the profound without flinching, but for him, unfortunately, something else goes very wrong. In the dramatic portrayal of how this error practically destroys him, Shakespeare hopes to impart the most important message of all.

But first, let us return to the ongoing dialogue between the Queen and Hamlet. The Queen has just asked Hamlet why the death of his father, being a common event, seems so particular with him.

Hamlet Seems, madam? Nay, it is. I know not 'seems.'
'Tis not alone my inky cloak, good mother,
Nor customary suits of solemn black,
Nor windy suspiration[32] of forced breath,
No, nor the fruitful river in the eye,
Nor the dejected haviour of the visage,
Together with all forms, moods, shapes of grief,
That can denote me truly. These indeed seem,
For they are actions that a man might play;
But I have that within which passes show,
These but the trappings and the suits of woe.

While this passage stresses the depth of Hamlet's grief, it is also the first hint of a theme that will echo repeatedly through the play—the projection of false appearances.

King 'Tis sweet and commendable in your nature, Hamlet,
To give these mourning duties to your father,
But you must know your father lost a father,
That father lost, lost his; and the survivor bound
In filial obligation for some term
To do obsequious sorrow.

The King expresses the basic truth that everyone dies, but he believes that mourning is merely an obsequious duty. This is in complete contradiction to Hamlet's statement that his appearance of sorrow is merely "the trappings and suits of woe," and that what is real is within. The contrast between the King and Hamlet is evident. The King continues:

---

[32] **suspiration** sighing

King But to persever
In obstinate condolement[33] is a course
Of impious stubbornness, 'tis unmanly grief,
It shows a will most incorrect to heaven,
A heart unfortified, a mind impatient,
An understanding simple and unschooled;
For what we know must be, and is as common
As any the most vulgar thing to sense,
Why should we in our peevish opposition
Take it to heart? Fie, 'tis a fault to heaven,
A fault against the dead, a fault to nature,
To reason most absurd; whose common theme
Is death of fathers, and who still hath cried
From the first corse[34] till he that died today,
'This must be so.'

Shakespeare has the King reiterating the common reaction to death: Since death is common, why take it to heart? Yet the question answers itself. We should take it to heart for the very reason that it is common. Here lies an essential ingredient to spirituality. The spiritual person confronts reality, accepts the truth, and seeks out a resolution. The mundane person simply ignores the truth.

The message in *Hamlet* targets the average person, since the average person often fails to accept the inevitability of death. While we readily admit that "everyone dies," we tend to behave as though we will live forever; we have not actually *realized* we will die. In the Indian epic *The Mahabharata*, one of the heroes, Yudhistira, was posed with the question: "What is the greatest wonder?" Yudhistira's reply was: "Day after day and hour after hour, people die and corpses are carried along, yet the onlookers never realize that they are also to die one day, but think they will live forever. This is the greatest wonder of the world."[35]

---

[33] **condolement** grief

[34] **corse** corpse (in the Bible, "the first corse" would be Abel, murdered by his brother, Cain)

[35] Excerpt is from *The Mahabhrata* (A Shortened Modern Prose Version) by R. K. Narayan (William Heinemann Ltd, 1978).

The failure to confront our own mortality is one reason why we have missed the meaning of *Hamlet* for so long. Most of us would actually accept the King's words as being true and sensible: "Death cannot be helped—why concern ourselves with it?" That is how we often think. Even when Shakespeare emphasizes its absurdity with the King and Queen's frivolous response (by their hasty marriage), we may merely condemn their marriage and still fail to recognize their denial of death. The play, however, reveals that it *is* Shakespeare's intent to make the denial of mortality a key issue. He creates a thematic resonance concerning it, and no other Shakespearean play comes even remotely close to *Hamlet* in the number of references to death and its reality.

In this scene, we can see that neither the King nor the Queen seriously accepts the truth of their personal mortality. They are the first two characters we encounter who portray the different methods used to hide from the profound.

Among them, the King, Claudius, is the most deluded of all. He completely gives way to his evil impulses in his quest for power, prestige, wealth, and all the mundane pleasures of life, as though any of these can help him in the end. He has deliberately barred the truth from himself. Without a total change to his lifestyle and motivation in life, he will be unable to accept the truth staring at him. In a sense, he lives almost in a state of drunken stupor, steadfastly refusing to see things as they are.

The Queen, Gertrude, exhibits a different way of hiding from the profound. As suggested by her hasty remarriage, she seeks refuge in the sensual pleasures and comforts of life. She shields herself from the knocks and trials of life by complying readily with whatever ensures her comfort and physical well-being. She, too, is deluded because there is no way she can avoid the profound in the end. But while she still can, she also steadfastly refuses to see things as they are.

Back at the royal court in Denmark, the King and Queen next request Hamlet to stay with them in Elsinore rather than return to school at Wittenburg. Hamlet readily agrees.

King Why, 'tis a loving and a fair reply.
Be as ourself in Denmark. Madam, come.
This gentle and unforced accord of Hamlet

Sits smiling to my heart; in grace whereof
No jocund health that Denmark drinks today
But the great cannon to the clouds shall tell,
And the King's rouse[36] the heavens shall bruit[37] again,
Re-speaking earthly thunder. Come away.

The King is certainly far removed from any sense of bereavement; he is, in fact, in a celebratory mood. This brings into stark contrast the first soliloquy of Hamlet (after the King and Queen leave), which reemphasizes how readily the King and Queen distance themselves and hide from the reality of death.

Hamlet Oh that this too too solid flesh would melt,
Thaw and resolve itself into a dew,
Or that the Everlasting had not fixed
His canon 'gainst self-slaughter. Oh God! God!
How weary, stale, flat, and unprofitable
Seem to me all the uses of this world!
Fie on't, ah fie! 'Tis an unweeded garden
That grows to seed; things rank and gross in nature
Possess it merely. That it should come to this!
But two months dead—nay, not so much, not two—
So excellent a king, that was to this
Hyperion[38] to a satyr;[39] so loving to my mother
That he might not beteem[40] the winds of heaven
Visit her face too roughly. Heaven and earth!
Must I remember? Why, she would hang on him
As if increase of appetite had grown
By what it fed on; and yet within a month—
Let me not think on't! Frailty, thy name is woman!
A little month, or ere those shoes were old
With which she followed my poor father's body,

---

36 **rouse** drink

37 **bruit** proclaim noisily

38 **Hyperion** the sun god

39 **satyr** half man half goat

40 **beteem** allow

Like Niobe,[41] all tears—why she, even she—
Oh God! A beast that wants discourse of reason[42]
Would have mourned longer—married with my uncle,
My father's brother—but no more like my father
Than I to Hercules. Within a month,
Ere yet the salt of most unrighteous tears
Had left the flushing in her galled eyes,
She married. Oh most wicked speed! To post
With such dexterity to incestuous sheets!
It is not, nor it cannot come to good.
But break, my heart, for I must hold my tongue.

Hamlet has the courage to face reality without flinching; he fully accepts the pain of bereavement and the reality of death. This, as we have noted, is an important requirement on the spiritual path. Yet we already sense that something has gone wrong, for Hamlet's despair has reached suicidal proportions. What has interfered with his process of spiritual development is quite evident: Hamlet is condemning his mother for her hasty remarriage.

We may feel that he is justified in doing so, for a remarriage with such haste is usually deemed an unworthy act. Yet it is exactly Shakespeare's intention to show that the act of condemning another, regardless of how justified it is, wrecks our spiritual development. This is typical of Shakespeare. To make us realize the error of a certain action, he will provide the most justifiable reason for it, and then proceed nonetheless to make us feel that it is wrong, and, more importantly, to show us why it is wrong.

While we should certainly be mindful of the moral correctness of any action and try to guide others to what is right, the act of condemning another goes beyond that, becoming a hostile act of separation that demarcates "others" from the "self." This separation harms our spiritual development, for it runs counter to the spiritual path, which is a path of the

---

41 **Niobe** mythical mother who wept endlessly for her slain children

42 **wants discourse of reason** lacks reasoning power

heart, a path of compassion that leads to a sense of unity and the realization of the oneness[43] of all.

Hamlet ends his soliloquy as Horatio, Marcellus, and Barnardo arrive. After a warm greeting, especially with Horatio who is a friend from Wittenburg, Hamlet asks why he is in Elsinore.

Horatio My lord, I came to see your father's funeral.

Hamlet I prithee do not mock me, fellow student.
I think it was to see my mother's wedding.

Horatio Indeed, my lord, it followed hard upon.

Hamlet Thrift, thrift, Horatio. The funeral baked meats
Did coldly furnish forth the marriage tables.

We experience again Hamlet's propensity for sharp, witty remarks that is almost a form of bitter self-mockery at his own tormented state of mind. The conversation then focuses on Hamlet's late father:

Horatio I saw him once; he was a goodly king.

Hamlet He was a man, take him for all in all;
I shall not look upon his like again.

Horatio My lord, I think I saw him yesternight.

Hamlet Saw? Who?

Horatio My lord, the king your father.

Hamlet The king my father?

Horatio Season your admiration[44] for a while
With an attent ear till I may deliver
Upon the witness of these gentlemen
This marvel to you.

Hamlet For God's love, let me hear!

---

43 "Oneness" here does not mean that we all become, and function as, a single homogeneous entity. The term is more to be taken in the sense of a transcendent realization of nonseparation.

44 **season your admiration** control your wonder

Horatio relates the events of the previous night, and Hamlet thus learns of the appearance of his father's ghost. He questions Horatio closely about the event:

Hamlet Did you not speak to it?

Horatio My lord, I did,
But answer made it none. Yet once methought
It lifted up its head and did address
Itself to motion like as it would speak.
But even then the morning cock crew loud,
And at the sound it shrunk in haste away
And vanished from our sight.

We are reminded once again of the nature of the ghost—that it is no enlightened being and that we must treat its advice accordingly. After obtaining further details from Horatio about the encounter, Hamlet resolves to meet the ghost of his father:

Hamlet I will watch tonight.
Perchance 'twill walk again.

Horatio I warrant it will.

Hamlet If it assume my noble father's person,
I'll speak to it though hell itself should gape
And bid me hold my peace.

As well as an indication of his willingness to confront the profound in whatever form, we also have a glimpse of Hamlet's bold and impetuous nature. He hardly seems prone to delaying his actions. We must remember this when the question of his delay in taking revenge comes up.

The scene closes with Hamlet, now alone, revealing his premonition that something evil had transpired:

Hamlet My father's spirit—in arms! All is not well.
I doubt[45] some foul play. Would the night were come.
Till then sit still, my soul. Foul deeds will rise,
Though all the earth o'erwhelm them, to men's eyes.

---

45 **doubt** suspect

Scene 3

The emotional impact of the next scene again depends on the previous one, for there is a marked contrast between the intensity and the superficiality of the two scenes. Here, we also see how three other characters portray our different ways of hiding from the profound.

The scene opens with a conversation between Ophelia and Laertes, who is preparing to embark for France. Their conversation soon touches on Hamlet:

Laertes For Hamlet, and the trifling of his favour,
Hold it a fashion and a toy in blood,[46]
A violet in the youth of primy[47] nature,
Forward, not permanent, sweet, not lasting,
The perfume and suppliance of a minute,[48]
No more.

Ophelia No more but so?

Laertes Think it no more.

Laertes thus urges his sister to resist the romantic advances of Hamlet for the following reason:

Laertes Perhaps he loves you now,
And now no soil nor cautel[49] doth besmirch
The virtue of his will; but you must fear,
His greatness weighed,[50] his will is not his own.
For he himself is subject to his birth:
He may not, as unvalued persons do,
Carve for himself, for on his choice depends
The safety and health of this whole state;
And therefore must his choice be circumscribed
Unto the voice and yielding of that body
Whereof he is the head.

---

46 **toy in blood** whim of passion

47 **primy** of springtime

48 **perfume and suppliance of a minute** momentary diversion

49 **cautel** deceit

50 **greatness weighed** high position considered

Laertes contends that Hamlet will be constrained in his choice of partner because he is heir to the throne of Denmark. We shall see, later, that Polonius gives exactly the opposite reasoning, and yet comes to the same conclusion that Ophelia should be wary of Hamlet.

The real reason for Laertes's concern is probably more in what he says later:

Laertes Then weigh what loss your honour may sustain
If with too credent[51] ear you list his songs,
Or lose your heart, or your chaste treasure open
To his unmastered importunity.
Fear it, Ophelia, fear it, my dear sister,
And keep you in the rear of your affection
Out of the shot and danger of desire.
The chariest[52] maid is prodigal enough
If she unmask her beauty to the moon.
Virtue itself scapes not calumnious strokes.

Laertes's main concern appears to be the risk to Ophelia's good name and, hence, to his family reputation. This is a glimpse of Laertes's character. He avoids the profound by focusing instead on his reputation and the approval of society and consistently tailors his own behavior to suit the public eye (a characteristic eventually used by the King to manipulate him). This, of course, is a common trait among us and may even appear a virtue. But if we truly confront the profound, it quickly reveals itself as a shallow and irrelevant concern.

It is exactly to show the petty nature of such concerns that Shakespeare places this scene here. It follows immediately after we witness Hamlet in despair over his father's death and his mother's hasty remarriage, and later in preparation to meet the ghost of his father. The profundity of that scene and the pettiness of this one are in dramatic contrast. It is painful to witness Laertes and, later, Polonius denying the despairing Hamlet the only thing that may have actually saved him. And this, all because of the petty fear for their family reputation, even when there is not the slightest evidence that Hamlet's courtship is insincere.

---

51 **credent** credulous

52 **chariest** most modest

Under these circumstances, Ophelia's response, now and later to Polonius, reveals much about her character.

Laertes Be wary then: best safety lies in fear.
Youth to itself rebels, though none else near.

Ophelia I shall the effect of this good lesson keep
As watchman to my heart.

Ophelia is the passive, obedient one who believes she can avoid the shocks of life by staying within the norms of society and following all the rules. She lacks the spirit of a seeker; when she is confronted with the profound later, she truly disintegrates.

Polonius arrives and finds Laertes still not underway. He takes the opportunity to present him a list of precepts:

Polonius Yet here, Laertes? Aboard, aboard for shame.
The wind sits in the shoulder of your sail,
And you are stayed for. There, my blessing with thee.
And these few precepts in thy memory
Look thou character.[53] Give thy thoughts no tongue,
Nor any unproportioned[54] thought his act.
Be thou familiar,[55] but by no means vulgar;
The friends thou hast, and their adoption tried,
Grapple them unto thy soul with hoops of steel,
But do not dull thy palm with entertainment
Of each new hatched, unfledged comrade. Beware
Of entrance to a quarrel, but being in,
Bear't that th'opposed may beware of thee.
Give every man thy ear, but few thy voice;
Take each man's censure, but reserve thy judgment.
Costly thy habit[56] as thy purse can buy,
But not expressed in fancy; rich, not gaudy,
For the apparel oft proclaims the man,

---

53 **character** inscribe

54 **unproportioned** unbalanced

55 **familiar** sociable

56 **habit** clothes

And they in France of the best rank and station
Are of a most select and generous chief in that.
Neither a borrower nor a lender be,
For loan oft loses both itself and friend,
And borrowing dulls the edge of husbandry.[57]

Every bit of advice in this list is relevant only for mundane matters and does not even begin to address the kind of problems facing Hamlet. The precepts are petty in nature. We cannot imagine Jesus, Buddha, or any other spiritual sage saying these proverbs.

This long string of advice reveals much about the character of Polonius. He is a man mainly concerned with the affairs of the mundane world. Polonius thus represents the pseudo-intellect who refuses to confront the profound and hides behind a dense wall of intellectual arguments and analyses, none of which addresses anything of a spiritual nature.

It was a tradition of the period for a father to advise a son leaving on his travels, and Shakespeare merely rephrases current precepts for Polonius. Nonetheless, they still characterize Polonius as a shallow pseudo-intellect hiding from the profound. The messages in Shakespeare's plays target the average population, the norm of society. If such precepts were common at the time, it was probably Shakespeare's aim to deliberately comment on them in this way by having Polonius deliver them.

Let us now look at the last advice of Polonius, which is worth separate consideration.

Polonius This above all: to thine own self be true,
And it must follow as the night the day
Thou canst not then be false to any man.

This is true enough, but Polonius, as we shall see, fails to heed his own words, words that echo one of the main themes in the play—the question of being honest both to ourselves and to others. Being true to our own self essentially means facing up to reality, to the inevitable, and to the profound. If we are unable to do this, we will fill our lives with petty, irrelevant concerns and deceitful conduct, both to ourselves and to others.

In the play, Shakespeare provides us with a thematic resonance of exactly this phenomenon. He presents a catalogue of repeated violations

---

57 **husbandry** thrift

of honesty both to one's own self and to others—violations by practically all the main characters, including Polonius. Only Hamlet courageously faces his mortality and the profound. Unfortunately, he fails to be honest to himself in another way, and also ends up being false to others.

After Laertes leaves, Polonius learns from Ophelia that they had been discussing Hamlet. Polonius asks about their relationship; and when Ophelia protests that Hamlet has been honorable in his courtship, Polonius cynically rejects it all as tricks and traps:

Ophelia My lord, he hath importuned me with love
In honourable fashion.

Polonius Ay, fashion you may call it. Go to, go to.

Ophelia And hath given countenance[58] to his speech, my lord,
With almost all the holy vows of heaven.

Polonius Ay, springes[59] to catch woodcocks![60] I do know,
When the blood burns, how prodigal the soul
Lends the tongue vows. These blazes, daughter,
Giving more light than heat, extinct in both,
Even in their promise as it is a-making,
You must not take for fire.

Polonius now gives his reason why Ophelia should be wary of Hamlet. It directly contradicts the reason Laertes gives:

Polonius For Lord Hamlet,
Believe so much in him that he is young,
And with a larger tether may he walk
Than may be given you.

While Laertes feels that Hamlet, being the heir to the throne, will be constrained in his actions, Polonius says exactly the opposite. Nonetheless they both advise Ophelia against him, and Polonius goes further with a command to his daughter:

---

58 **countenance** authority

59 **springes** snares

60 **woodcocks** proverbially stupid birds

Polonius I would not, in plain terms, from this time forth
Have you so slander[61] any moment leisure
As to give words or talk with the Lord Hamlet.
Look to't, I charge you. Come your ways.

Ophelia I shall obey, my lord.

In such meek fashion, with these simple words, Ophelia cuts perhaps the only lifeline left to the already distraught Hamlet and abandons him to his fate. The pain her betrayal causes is almost tangible.

If Polonius is unreasonable, Ophelia must appear even more so. But she is meek and seeks to avoid the harsh realities of life by sheltering under the tame submission to convention. Ironically, her actions probably accelerate her eventual confrontation with the profound, something she is totally unprepared for.

61 **slander** disgrace

Scene 4

Scene 4 brings us back to the battlements of the castle wall in the dark of night. Hamlet now awaits the appearance of the ghost, and we are once again immersed in an aura of mystery, awaiting an encounter with the beyond. It is around midnight.

Hamlet The air bites shrewdly, it is very cold.

Horatio It is a nipping and an eager[62] air.

Hamlet What hour now?

Horatio I think it lacks of twelve.

Marcellus No, it is struck.

Horatio Indeed? I heard it not.
It then draws near the season
Wherein the spirit held his wont to walk.

The suspense builds. In the distance, a flourish of trumpets and the sound of two pieces of ordnance firing prompt Horatio's question:

Horatio What does this mean, my lord?

Hamlet The King doth wake tonight and takes his rouse,[63]
Keeps wassail,[64] and the swagg'ring upspring[65] reels;
And, as he drains his draughts of Rhenish[66] down,
The kettle-drum and trumpet thus bray out
The triumph of his pledge.[67]

The sound of celebrations in the distance intensifies the isolation at the castle wall. We are now truly on the outside, beyond the coziness of mundane distractions, with the night skies stretching the horizons before us. Now we are on the cutting edge between the known and the vast beyond.

---

62 **eager** sharp

63 **takes his rouse** carouses

64 **wassail** carousal

65 **upspring** a dance

66 **Rhenish** Rhine wine

67 **pledge** toast

The sound of the King celebrating also brings into sharp contrast the characters of Hamlet and Claudius. One is preparing to face the profound, while the other is attempting to drown out any hint of it in wanton revelry.

Horatio enquires of Hamlet whether drinking and revelry of this kind is customary. Hamlet responds by criticizing this drunkenness as a tradition that damages the nation's reputation and belittles its achievements. He then generalizes this effect to include any vice and explains how a single defect can overwhelm all of one's virtues:

Hamlet So, oft it chances in particular men
That for some vicious mole[68] of nature in them,
As in their birth, wherein they are not guilty
(Since nature cannot choose his origin),
By the o'ergrowth of some complexion,[69]
Oft breaking down the pales[70] and forts of reason,
Or by some habit, that too much o'erleavens[71]
The form of plausive[72] manners—that these men,
Carrying, I say, the stamp of one defect,
Being Nature's livery or Fortune's star,
His virtues else, be they as pure as grace,
As infinite as man may undergo,
Shall in the general censure take corruption
From that particular fault. The dram[73] of evil
Doth all the noble substance often dout
To his own scandal.

The actual wording of the last sentence is problematic because of a corruption in the published text, but the sense is clear: A small amount of something bad ruins all the noble substance.

Shakespeare has Hamlet say these words just before the ghost appears before him for a reason. The words ironically indicate exactly what will

68 **mole** blemish

69 **complexion** natural tendency

70 **pales** palisades, fences

71 **o'erleavens** mixes with thoroughly (as leaven works on the entire dough)

72 **plausive** pleasing

73 **dram** minute amount

happen to Hamlet himself because of the ghost. Hamlet is intelligent, courageous, and sensitive, with all the makings of a true philosopher king. Yet something goes very amiss with him, and it is exactly at this point that he encounters the poison that practically destroys him.

The ghost now appears.

Horatio Look, my lord, it comes.

Hamlet Angels and ministers of grace defend us!
Be thou a spirit of health or goblin damned,
Bring with thee airs from heaven or blasts from hell,
Be thy intents wicked or charitable,
Thou comest in such a questionable shape
That I will speak to thee.

Like Horatio in Scene 1, Hamlet questions the nature of the ghost, particularly whether it brings good or evil. Nevertheless, Hamlet feels compelled to proceed, compelled to seek the unknown, and he does so without flinching:

Hamlet I'll call thee Hamlet,
King, father, royal Dane. Oh answer me!
Let me not burst in ignorance, but tell
Why thy canonized[74] bones, hearsed in death,
Have burst their cerements;[75] why the sepulcher
Wherein we saw thee quietly inurned
Hath op'd his ponderous and marble jaws
To cast thee up again. What may this mean,
That thou, dead corse, again in complete steel
Revisits thus the glimpses of the moon,
Making night hideous and we fools of nature
So horridly to shake our disposition
With thoughts beyond the reaches of our souls?
Say why is this? Wherefore? What should we do?

The ghost beckons Hamlet to follow; Horatio and Marcellus fear for his safety, but Hamlet is determined to learn from the ghost.

---

74 **canonized** consecrated

75 **cerements** grave-clothes

Horatio It beckons you to go away with it,
As if it some impartment[76] did desire
To you alone.

Marcellus Look with what courteous action
It waves you to a more removed ground.
But do not go with it.

Horatio No, by no means.

Hamlet It will not speak. Then I will follow it.

Horatio Do not, my lord.

Hamlet Why, what should be the fear?
I do not set my life at a pin's fee,
And for my soul, what can it do to that,
Being a thing immortal as itself?
It waves me forth again. I'll follow it.

Hamlet clearly demonstrates his courage and ability to face the profound. He barely pauses to consider the danger and rushes boldly to confront the unknown. He certainly does not appear to be a man prone to delaying his actions from fear or lack of will.

Now, through the words of Horatio, Shakespeare presents us with a brilliant image of what the ghost is about to do to Hamlet, a sensitive man with the courage to confront the profound:

Horatio What if it tempt you toward the flood, my lord,
Or to the dreadful summit of the cliff
That beetles[77] o'er his base into the sea,
And there assume some other horrible form
Which might deprive your sovereignty of reason[78]
And draw you into madness? Think of it:
The very place puts toys[79] of desperation,
Without more motive, into every brain
That looks so many fathoms to the sea
And hears it roar beneath.

---

76 **impartment** communication

77 **beetles** projects out, overhangs

78 **deprive your sovereignity of reason** remove the supremacy of your reason

79 **toys** whims, fancies

A confrontation with the profound is like standing fully exposed on the edge of a great abyss, a stark encounter with the vast reality beyond, and we must be prepared for it. We must face it with the qualities of universal love and compassion—otherwise it may well put "toys of desperation" into our brain. This, then, is the problem for Hamlet. He is confronting the profound, but instead of meeting it with the spiritual qualities of love and compassion, he tragically accepts the burden of a dangerous poison—the poison of revenge. The will to vengeance together with a mind that fully accepts the truth of our mortal state is a terrifying combination, leading to a fatalistic view of utter desolation. This, then, becomes the tragic consequence of the ghost's dreadful injunction to Hamlet.

The scene continues with a dramatic depiction of Hamlet's courage in facing the unknown. He shakes off the restraints of his two friends and plunges on imperiously. He is compelled to go.

Hamlet It waves me still.
Go on, I'll follow thee.

Marcellus You shall not go, my lord.

Hamlet Hold off your hands.

Horatio Be ruled; you shall not go.

Hamlet My fate cries out
And makes each petty artery in this body
As hardy as the Nemean lion's[80] nerve.
Still am I called. Unhand me, gentlemen.
By heaven, I'll make a ghost of him that lets[81] me.
I say away! Go on, I'll follow thee.

The ghost leaves with Hamlet, and the scene ends with Horatio and Marcellus resolving to follow them.

---

80 **Nemean lion** mythical lion slain by Hercules

81 **lets** hinders

Scene 5

The ghost enters with Hamlet, and the confrontation with the beyond continues.

Hamlet Whither wilt thou lead me? Speak, I'll go no further.

Ghost Mark me.

Hamlet I will.

Ghost My hour is almost come
When I to sulph'rous and tormenting flames
Must render up myself.

Hamlet Alas, poor ghost.

The very first words of the ghost inform us that he is no angel. Shakespeare reminds us that the spirit is not one whose counsel we should take as infallible wisdom. There is nothing, in fact, to suggest that he is less deluded than any of us.

Ghost Pity me not, but lend thy serious hearing
To what I shall unfold.

Hamlet Speak, I am bound to hear.

Ghost So art thou to revenge when thou shalt hear.

Hamlet What?

Ghost I am thy father's spirit,
Doomed for a certain term to walk the night,
And for the day confined to fast in fires,
Till the foul crimes done in my days of nature
Are burnt and purged away.

Shakespeare stresses again that the ghost is no angel but rather a spirit still needing to have his crimes purged. To ensure that we do not miss this, Shakespeare even gets him to relate how terrible his temporary state of purging is.

Ghost But that I am forbid
To tell the secrets of my prison-house,
I could a tale unfold whose lightest word
Would harrow up thy soul, freeze thy young blood,

Make thy two eyes like stars start from their spheres,
Thy knotted and combined locks to part,
And each particular hair to stand on end
Like quills upon the fretful porpentine.[82]
But this eternal blazon[83] must not be
To ears of flesh and blood.

Shakespeare goes to extreme lengths to emphasize that the ghost is no enlightened being. At the end of this scene, he virtually forces us to experience it emotionally. He has a good reason for this: It is crucial to the message of the play that we understand this point, for it is the ghost's terrible mandate for Hamlet to wreak revenge that eventually destroys him spiritually.

The ghost now reveals his secret:

Ghost List, list, oh, list!
If thou didst ever thy dear father love—

Hamlet Oh, God!

Ghost Revenge his foul and most unnatural murder.

Hamlet Murder!

Ghost Murder most foul, as in the best it is,
But this most foul, strange and unnatural.

Hamlet Haste me to know't, that I with wings as swift
As meditation[84] or the thoughts of love
May sweep to my revenge.

Hamlet's initial reaction is to swiftly avenge his father, a reaction probably brought on by the sudden shock of the ghost's revelation. But, as we know, it does not turn out that way, although the ghost certainly expected it to.

---

82 **porpentine** porcupine

83 **eternal blazon** revelation of the secrets of eternity

84 **meditation** thought

Ghost I find thee apt;
And duller shouldst thou be than the fat weed
That roots itself in ease on Lethe[85] wharf,
Wouldst thou not stir in this. Now, Hamlet, hear.
'Tis given out that, sleeping in my orchard,
A serpent stung me; so the whole ear of Denmark
Is by a forged process[86] of my death
Rankly abused; but know, thou noble youth,
The serpent that did sting thy father's life
Now wears his crown.

Hamlet Oh my prophetic soul! My uncle!

Hamlet, it appears, already had intuitive misgivings about his uncle, even before the ghost's revelation.

Ghost Ay, that incestuous, that adulterate beast,
With witchcraft of his wit, with traitorous gifts—
Oh wicked wit, and gifts that have the power
So to seduce!—won to his shameful lust
The will of my most seeming-virtuous queen.
Oh Hamlet, what a falling off was there,
From me, whose love was of that dignity
That it went hand in hand even with the vow
I made to her in marriage; and to decline
Upon a wretch whose natural gifts were poor
To those of mine!
But virtue, as it never will be moved,
Though lewdness court it in a shape of heaven,
So lust, though to a radiant angel linked,
Will sate itself[87] in a celestial bed
And prey on garbage.

The ghost thus characterizes the Queen as one basically driven by lust into a hasty remarriage. In the play, Gertrude hides from the profound by securing her own physical comfort and well-being from which she derives

85 **Lethe** river of forgetfulness in Hades

86 **process** account

87 **sate itself** become satiated

a false sense of security. Later, even after being informed of the evil nature of Claudius, she continues to stand by him tamely and finally realizes her error only after becoming an accidental victim of his treachery.

Back at the scene on the castle wall, the ghost now relates how Hamlet's father was poisoned. While he was sleeping in his orchard, Claudius had stolen in and poured a vial of hebenon into his ear, curdling his blood and causing his body to break out in loathsome crusts. In this way was he murdered without an opportunity to repent his transgressions. Thus does the ghost present to Hamlet the poison, the dram of evil, which eventually ruins the noble substance within him. It is the poison of revenge.

Hamlet now has a justifiable cause for revenge. It is hard to conceive of a better reason for vengeance. His father has been murdered in a cowardly manner, and the villain has even entered hastily into an incestuous relationship with his mother. It is, however, characteristic of Shakespeare to present his message this way: If revenge is wrong per se, it has to be wrong even under the most justifiable circumstances. So Shakespeare presents us with the most acceptable reason for vengeance and then proceeds to show us why it is wrong.

Shakespeare echoes the message of Jesus: "You have heard that it was said, 'An eye for an eye, and a tooth for a tooth.' But now I tell you: do not take revenge on someone who wrongs you. If anyone slaps you on the right cheek, let him slap your left cheek too." Difficult as it may sound, the advice of Jesus is also meant to apply here. Our actions, out of compassion, should always be based on helping others. Not only does killing Claudius for revenge solve nothing, it is wrong and positively harmful for another reason. In *Hamlet*, Shakespeare demonstrates the reason. In fact, he makes us live through the experience.

The ghost now continues:

Ghost If thou has nature[88] in thee, bear it not,
Let not the royal bed of Denmark be
A couch for luxury and damned incest.
But howsoever thou pursuest this act,
Taint not thy mind nor let thy soul contrive
Against thy mother aught. Leave her to heaven,
And to those thorns that in her bosom lodge
To prick and sting her. Fare thee well at once:

---

88 **nature** natural feelings

The glow-worm shows the matin[89] to be near
And 'gins to pale his uneffectual fire.
Adieu, adieu, adieu. Remember me.

The ghost thus ends with an injunction for Hamlet to avenge him. Although he tells Hamlet to leave his mother "to heaven," this warning does little to stop Hamlet's condemnation of her. His bitter condemnation of his mother only adds to the terrible poison of revenge, and now the poison goes to work:

Hamlet Oh all you host of heaven! Oh earth! What else?
And shall I couple hell? Oh fie! Hold, hold, my heart,
And you, my sinews, grow not instant old,
But bear me stiffly up. Remember thee?
Ay, thou poor ghost, while memory holds a seat
In this distracted globe.[90] Remember thee?
Yea, from the table[91] of my memory
I'll wipe away all trivial fond[92] records,
All saws[93] of books, all forms, all pressures[94] past
That youth and observation copied there,
And thy commandment all alone shall live
Within the book and volume of my brain,
Unmixed with baser matter. Yes, by heaven!
Oh most pernicious woman!
Oh villain, villain, smiling damned villain!
My tables. Meet it is I set it down
That one may smile, and smile, and be a villain—
At least I may be sure it may be so in Denmark. [*Writes*]
So, uncle, there you are. Now to my word.
It is 'Adieu, adieu, remember me.'
I have sworn't.

---

89 **matin** morning

90 **globe** head

91 **table** writing tablet, notebook

92 **fond** foolish

93 **saws** sayings

94 **pressures** impressions

Hamlet has the courage to face the unknown and to seek the truth unflinchingly. If he follows this path with the ideals of love and compassion, new spiritual heights will open to him. Tragically, he chooses instead to transform his mind into one obsessed with avenging his father. This mind of bitterness and hatred has disastrous consequences. Hamlet, from this time on, remorselessly transforms into a different person: a cold, cynical, and tormented soul. Thus his new motto is appropriate: "Adieu, adieu, remember me." For, in effect, we are bidding Hamlet himself goodbye.

In so demonstrating why revenge is wrong, it may seem that Shakespeare does not give due consideration to justice. Surely Hamlet and the ghost have cause to seek redress. Without justice, how is the world a viable place in which to live? Yet Shakespeare does seem indifferent to poetic justice, particularly when it concerns punishment for the transgressor, a trait that is evident from a number of his other plays such as *The Tempest*, *Measure for Measure*, and *All's Well That Ends Well.* In all these plays, the wrongdoer virtually goes unpunished.

Why is Shakespeare so unconcerned with poetic justice? It is, in fact, the same reason why saints or bodhisattvas never demand justice. That is simply not their purpose; instead they seek to save all beings from suffering. Seeking justice is not necessary for this purpose. In any case, heaven or the law of karma will take care of justice. A saint or a bodhisattva need not be concerned with it.

We may argue, though, that justice is necessary for society to thrive. True, but this is for a society living for mundane ends. If our concern is to accomplish worldly goals, then we should be concerned with seeking justice. Without some rule of justice, favorable circumstances for achieving worldly ends may be jeopardized. Shakespeare realizes, however, that worldly ends do not solve the real problems of the world. They cannot cure the world of the suffering from sorrow, sickness, ageing, and death. We are deluding ourselves and refusing to face the profound if we ignore the fact that the goals of the mundane world cannot help here.

So we need to be clear about our motives. If we truly aim to help the world, we must embark on the spiritual path, come to terms with the truth, and develop love and compassion so that we may lead others to salvation. Seeking justice is irrelevant. Justice takes care of itself. We should seek only to save all beings, without any exception.

On a different point, we note that Hamlet's soliloquy above contains a curious emphasis on the idea that "one may smile, and smile, and be a villain." In fact, Hamlet takes pains to write this down, an act that seems out of place and noticeably jolts the flow of the drama. This effect, however, is exactly as Shakespeare intends, for he is deliberately drawing our attention to a recurring motif in the play. It is the motif in the thematic resonance centered on honesty or, rather, our lack of it; and it echoes in a negative way the words of Polonius: "To thine own self be true, and it must follow as the night the day, thou canst not then be false to any man."

The King—the one who may smile and smile—does the reverse as he practices the art of deception. He is being false to himself by refusing to face up to the profound and to the truth of his own mortality; in this state of delusion, he has then given in to his evil impulses. After being false to himself, it follows then that he will also be false to others.

The idea that "one may smile, and smile, and be a villain" also alludes to our lack of honesty in another way. It highlights our propensity to artificially beautify what is actually rotten as a means of hiding from the truth. Images symbolizing this propensity appear repeatedly in the play, creating another unmistakable, but related, thematic resonance.

Back on the castle platform, Horatio and Marcellus now find Hamlet. In a state of excitement, they ask him what transpired. Hesitantly, Hamlet begins to tell them:

Hamlet How say you then, would heart of man once think it—
But you'll be secret?

Hor., Mar. Ay, by heaven.

Hamlet There's never a villain dwelling in all Denmark
But he's an arrant knave.

Hamlet changes his mind about telling them midway through his sentence. "But he's an arrant knave" certainly was not what he had in mind when he began the sentence. Now he resists revealing anything further.

Horatio There needs no ghost, my lord, come from the grave
To tell us this.

Hamlet Why, right, you are i'th'right.
And so without more circumstance at all,

	I hold it fit that we shake hands and part, You as your business and desire shall point you— For every man hath business and desire, Such as it is; and for my own poor part, I will go pray.
Horatio	These are but wild and whirling words, my lord.
Hamlet	I am sorry they offend you, heartily— Yes faith, heartily.
Horatio	There's no offence, my lord.
Hamlet	Yes by Saint Patrick but there is, Horatio, And much offence too. Touching this vision here, It is an honest ghost, that let me tell you. For your desire to know what is between us, O'ermaster't as you may.

Hamlet cannot help but hint that something is very wrong, but he resists saying more. His reference to an "honest ghost" shows that, at this point at least, he believes the account of the ghost. Now follows the scene with the swearing ritual.

The reason for this long scene, occurring after the ghost had already given an adequate account of his murder, has previously puzzled critics. It is certainly not needed to move forward the play's action. However, if we understand the effect of the ghost's injunction on Hamlet, the reason for this scene is evident. It is a focused allegorical scene deliberately crafted by Shakespeare to make clear the nature of what transpired by providing us with a dramatic image of evil at work. The voice of the ghost echoes from below, the traditional location of hell, and the way Hamlet now addresses the ghost strongly hints at the devil. While the ghost may not be the devil himself, the effect he has on Hamlet is surely worthy of the devil.

This eerie scene, with Hamlet's mischievous jesting remarks coupled with the sinister call of the ghost from below to swear, has an unmistakably diabolical aura. The swearing ritual here is linked to the earlier oath of Hamlet to transform himself into an instrument of his father's revenge. The oaths are all to aid Hamlet on the path of vengeance.

Hamlet	And now, good friends, As you are friends, scholars, and soldiers, Give me one poor request.
Horatio	What is't, my lord? We will.
Hamlet	Never make known what you have seen tonight.
Hor., Mar.	My lord, we will not.
Hamlet	Nay, but swear't.
Horatio	In faith, my lord, not I.
Marcellus	Nor I, my lord, in faith.
Hamlet	Upon my sword.
Marcellus	We have sworn, my lord, already.
Hamlet	Indeed, upon my sword, indeed.
Ghost	[*Beneath*] Swear
Hamlet	Ah ha, boy, say'st thou so? Art thou there, truepenny?[95] Come on, you hear this fellow in the cellarage. Consent to swear.

Hamlet's wild jesting adds a touch of the burlesque to the scene, suggesting mischief. Also, the strange familiarity in the way he refers to the ghost is reminiscent of how the traditional stage Vice used to address the devil. The sinister term "fellow in the cellarage" again hints at the devil.

Horatio	Propose the oath, my lord.
Hamlet	Never to speak of this that you have seen. Swear by my sword.
Ghost	Swear. [*They swear*]
Hamlet	*Hic et ubique*? Then we'll shift our ground. Come hither, gentlemen, And lay your hands again upon my sword. Swear by my sword Never to speak of this that you have heard.
Ghost	Swear by his sword. [*They swear*]

95 **truepenny** honest fellow

Hamlet Well said, old mole. Canst work i'th'earth so fast?
A worthy pioneer![96] Once more remove, good friends.

Hic et ubique is Latin for "here and everywhere." Traditionally, only God and the devil can be "here and everywhere" all at once. That the entity down below has this ability is also suggested by Hamlet's rhetorical question: "Canst work i'th'earth so fast?"

Horatio Oh, day and night, but this is wondrous strange.

Hamlet And therefore as a stranger give it welcome.
There are more things in heaven and earth, Horatio,
Than are dreamt of in your philosophy.

This is a true statement and a crucial one. We should keep an open mind and be receptive to the deeper reality beyond the mundane. Otherwise, we close the door to understanding the real meaning of our lives, and to the profound truths that may, at this time, still be veiled from us.

The greatest fault of modern science is its inability to admit ignorance in areas where current scientific techniques cannot penetrate. There are many areas that conventional science cannot even begin to access, particularly those involving consciousness and the mind. The usual response of many scientists is to redefine the boundaries of what is to be taken as science as well as what is to be taken as fact. We must be wary of this tactic and not allow our minds to be locked in by what is essentially an act of deception designed to conceal ignorance. Therefore, to something wondrous and strange that comes our way, we should, in Hamlet's words, as a stranger give it welcome. There is much we have yet to learn.

Hamlet But come,
Here, as before, never, so help you mercy,
How strange or odd some'er I bear myself—
As I perchance hereafter shall think meet
To put an antic[97] disposition on—
That you, at such time seeing me, never shall,
With arms encumbered[98] thus, or this head-shake,

96 **pioneer** digger, miner

97 **antic** mad

98 **encumbered** folded

Or by pronouncing of some doubtful phrase,
As 'Well, we know,' or 'We could and if we would,'
Or 'If we list to speak,' or 'There be and if they might,'
Or such ambiguous giving out, to note
That you know aught of me—this do swear,
So grace and mercy at your most need help you.

Ghost Swear [*They swear*]

Hamlet Rest, rest, perturbed spirit!

Hamlet thus resolves to feign madness in order to avoid suspicion of his motive for revenge. Ironically, he is actually following the example of Claudius—the one who smiles and smiles, and is yet a villain—in putting up a false front to conceal a more sinister underlying truth. All these practices of being false to others ultimately stem from not being true to oneself in the first place. While Claudius is not being true to himself by refusing to face up to the profound and to the truth of his own mortality, Hamlet is not being true to himself for another reason. As we shall see, he is refusing to acknowledge his inner voice and deeper conscience.

Now, finally, after the third oath of secrecy, the long swearing ritual comes to an end. The reason for its prolonged length should now be evident. All the elements of the ritual are suggestively diabolical. The proceedings are conducted in the dark through the use of almost derisive remarks, while being urged on by the sinister cries of a ghost from below. And all the oaths are taken to aid a path of revenge. The whole ritual thus leaves us with an emotional impression that what transpires—the injunction to vengeance—is actually evil in nature.

As the scene draws to a close, the tragedy of his circumstances dawns on Hamlet.

Hamlet The time is out of joint. Oh, cursed spite,
That ever I was born to set it right!

2

Act II

Scene 1

The impact of the first scene in Act II depends on its immediately following the last scene of Act I, despite the apparent pause between Acts. *Hamlet* was not originally conceived as five Acts;[1] editors introduced the separate Acts later in the published version.

When the play is staged, the scenes flow one after another, and part of Shakespeare's artistry lies in the emotional impact of the new scene while the previous one is still fresh in mind. For this reason, every one of the final scenes of each Act in *Hamlet* must be linked to the opening scene of the next Act. If we artificially break the flow, we lose Shakespeare's intended effect.

Act II opens with a dialogue between Polonius and Reynaldo, and the contrast between the gravity of the preceding scene and the pettiness of what transpires now is striking. Polonius is giving instructions, concerning Laertes, to Reynaldo:

Polonius You shall do marvellous wisely, good Reynaldo,
Before you visit him, to make inquire
Of his behaviour.

Reynaldo My lord, I did intend it.

Polonius Marry, well said, very well said. Look you, sir,
Inquire me first what Danskers[2] are in Paris,

---

1 See Preface to Hamlet, by Harley Granville-Barker (Hill & Wang, 1957); also reprinted as "The Five Acts of the Editors" in Hamlet, A Norton Critical Edition (W. W. Norton & Co., 1992) pp.192-196.

2 **Danskers** Danes

And how, and who, what means, and where they keep,
What company, at what expense; and finding
By this encompassment[3] and drift of question
That they do know my son, come you more nearer
Than your particular demands[4] will touch it.
Take you as 'twere some distant knowledge of him,
As thus, 'I know his father, and his friends,
And in part him.' Do you mark this, Reynaldo?

Reynaldo Ay, very well, my lord.

Polonius 'And in part him. But,' you may say, 'not well;
But if't be he I mean, he's very wild,
Addicted so and so'—and there put on him
What forgeries[5] you please—marry none so rank
As may dishonour him—take heed of that—
But sir, such wanton, wild, and usual slips
As are companions noted and most known
To youth and liberty.

Polonius instructs Reynaldo on how to spy on his son, Laertes, and how to deviously ferret out gossip about him. He advises Reynaldo to suggest to others that Laertes had been indulging in gaming, drinking, fencing, swearing, quarrelling, or whoring to gain their confidence and elicit from them real accounts of his misbehavior.

Polonius Marry, sir, here's my drift,
And I believe it is a fetch of warrant.
You laying these slight sullies on my son,
As 'twere a thing a little soiled i'th'working,
Mark you,
Your party in converse, him you would sound,
Having ever seen in the prenominate[6] crimes
The youth you breathe of guilty, be assured

---

3 **encompassment** circling, talking around the subject

4 **particular demands** direct questions

5 **forgeries** inventions

6 **prenominate** already named

He closes[7] with you in this consequence[8]
'Good sir,' or so, or 'friend,' or 'gentleman,'
According to the phrase or the addition
Of man and country.

Reynaldo Very good, my lord.

In a subtle touch, Shakespeare emphasizes the pettiness of the whole proceedings by having Polonius lose his train of thought midway in his speech.

Polonius And then, sir, does a this—a does—what was I about to say? By the mass, I was about to say something. Where did I leave?

Reynaldo At 'closes in the consequence.'

Polonius At 'closes in the consequence,' ay, marry.
He closes thus: 'I know the gentleman,
I saw him yesterday,' or 'th'other day,'
Or then, or then, with such or such, 'and as you say,
There was a gaming,' 'there o'ertook in's rouse,'
'There falling out at tennis,' or perchance
'I saw him enter such a house of sale'—
Videlicet[9] a brothel, or so forth.

Given that all this has no bearing on the main action of the play, its protracted length has puzzled critics. Why does Shakespeare dwell so much on this dialogue, especially since nothing related to it appears later? We never hear of Reynaldo, or what he did with the instructions, ever again. What then is Shakespeare's purpose here?

This episode is actually a focused allegorical scene deliberately crafted to highlight recurring motifs already encountered in the play. One is the motif centered on the word "honesty," or rather, the lack of it. Polonius's scheme to ferret information about Laertes certainly lacks honesty, but Shakespeare's concern is the lack of honesty at a deeper level. This is also illustrated here by the character of Polonius. Polonius is concerned about

7 **closes** falls in

8 **in this consequence** in the following way

9 **videlicet** namely

Laertes harming the family reputation and goes to extreme lengths to investigate. He is preoccupied with petty intrigues of little consequence; thus he hides from the profound by focusing instead on matters irrelevant to the real issues of life. This is the lack of honesty that Shakespeare is drawing our attention to—our lack of honesty in facing the truth.

This episode also highlights the failure to follow Polonius's own advice to Laertes: "To thine own self be true, and it must follow as the night the day, thou canst not then be false to any man," which is another recurring motif. Like Claudius, Polonius is neither true to himself nor to others. He occupies himself in being false to others by petty intrigues and elaborate deceptions because he is false to himself in the first place as he steadfastly refuses to face the profound.

This focused allegorical scene also illustrates a third recurring motif: the process of artificially beautifying things to conceal the truth, in this case, to conceal Polonius's real intention of spying on Laertes. Again, Shakespeare is more concerned with our propensity to artificially beautify at a deeper level. We frequently use the act of deception to hide from the profound—we artificially beautify reality to conceal the truth.

And now, after instructing Reynaldo on how to beautify, and thus, hide his real intentions, Polonius even "beautifies" his own behavior:

Polonius See you now,
Your bait of falsehood takes this carp of truth;
And thus do we of wisdom and of reach,
With windlasses [10] and with assays of bias, [11]
By indirections find directions out.
So by my former lecture and advice
Shall you my son.

Polonius not only deludes himself by his refusal to accept reality but also believes he is being worldly wise.

This lack of honesty in facing the truth, as well as our propensity to falsely beautify reality, brings up a related question that forms another thematic resonance in the play: Are we mad in behaving this way? With

---

10 **windlasses** roundabout methods

11 **assays of bias** indirect attempts (from the game of bowls: bias refers to the curved course of the bowl)

immaculate timing, Shakespeare now introduces this issue with the question of Hamlet's "madness." After Reynaldo leaves, Ophelia enters, distressed by Hamlet's unusual behavior:

Polonius	How now, Ophelia, what's the matter?
Ophelia	Oh, my lord, my lord, I have been so affrighted.
Polonius	With what, i'th'name of God?
Ophelia	My lord, as I was sewing in my closet, Lord Hamlet, with his doublet[12] all unbraced,[13] No hat upon his head, his stockings fouled, Ungartered and down-gyved[14] to his ankle, Pale as his shirt, his knees knocking each other, And with a look so piteous in purport[15] As if he had been loosed out of hell To speak of horrors, he comes before me.
Polonius	Mad for thy love?
Ophelia	My lord, I do not know, But truly, I do fear it.
Polonius	What said he?
Ophelia	He took me by the wrist and held me hard. Then goes he to the length of all his arm, And with his other hand thus o'er his brow He falls to such perusal of my face As he would draw it. Long stayed he so. At last, a little shaking of mine arm, And thrice his head thus waving up and down, He raised a sigh so piteous and profound As it did seem to shatter all his bulk And end his being. That done, he lets me go, And with his head over his shoulder turned

12 **doublet** jacket

13 **unbraced** unlaced

14 **down-gyved** fallen down, like gives or fetters on a prisoner's legs

15 **purport** expression

He seemed to find his way without his eyes,
For out o'doors he went without their helps,
And to the last bended their light on me.

Was this a genuine reaction of Hamlet or part of his plan to feign madness? Or was it a mixture of both? Since this is the first we hear of Hamlet after his resolve to put on an "antic disposition," we naturally associate this speech with feigned madness. Yet there is too much suggestion of a shattered love in Hamlet's reactions for us to ignore the possibility that his reaction may have been genuine.

In the end, there is no clear answer, but the ambiguity is deliberate. By leaving it obscure, Shakespeare blurs the line between sanity and madness. Is Hamlet merely feigning madness, or is part of it real? What actually constitutes madness? More to the point: Who is, in fact, mad?

This last question is highly relevant. Hamlet is the only one courageously facing the profound truths of life. Polonius, on the other hand, deludes himself with trivial concerns. Is he then not mad? The King obviously also refuses to accept the inevitability of death. He indulges in evil purely to increase the enjoyment of his limited life and then tries to drown all hints of the profound in drunken revelry. Is he not mad? The Queen succumbs to lust and her desire to secure the comforts of life; she remarries with unwarranted haste, ignoring the profundity of death, even when her husband had just died. Is she also not mad?

The same question can be extended to others in the play, including Laertes, Rosencrantz, Guildenstern, and, especially, Ophelia. It is particularly pertinent to Ophelia, for in the end, she does become undoubtedly mad. Yet are there not indications of madness in her even now? Ophelia believes she can hide from the traumas of life by conforming to conventional mores playing the role of the obedient daughter. This delusion soon gets shattered, plunging her to a stark confrontation with the truth. Because she is totally unprepared, she disintegrates.

Since those in the play are not too different from us, we also need to ask ourselves: Are we not mad? In not facing our mortality and in hiding from the profound, we are, at the very least, deluding ourselves. We may appear sane only because we are all equally mad. As Yudhistira says in *The Mahabhrata*, regarding the widespread denial that we are going to die one day, "This is the greatest wonder of the world."

Back in the play, Polonius now hastily concludes that Hamlet's apparent madness is the result of spurned love:

Polonius Come, go with me, I will go seek the King.
This is the very ecstasy of love,
Whose violent property fordoes[16] itself
And leads the will to desperate undertakings
As oft as any passion under heaven
That does afflict our natures, I am sorry—
What, have you given him any hard words of late?

Ophelia No, my good lord, but as you did command,
I did repel his letters and denied
His access to me.

Here is clear evidence of Ophelia's character. She tamely obeys Polonius's instructions to the letter without questioning their wisdom, even when Polonius is not around to observe her actions.

Polonius That hath made him mad.
I am sorry that with better heed and judgment
I had not quoted[17] him. I feared he did but trifle
And meant to wrack thee. But beshrew my jealousy![18]
By heaven, it is as proper to[19] our age
To cast beyond ourselves[20] in our opinions
As it is common for the younger sort
To lack discretion.

The irony of this last statement is that, even while saying it, Polonius is still casting beyond himself in his opinions. The scene ends with Polonius hurrying to present the King with his explanation for Hamlet's madness. The King, as we shall see, is not convinced.

---

16 **fordoes** destroys

17 **quoted** noted, observed

18 **beshrew my jealousy** shame upon my suspicions

19 **proper to** characteristic of

20 **cast beyond ourselves** to go too far

Scene 2

In this scene, we meet Rosencrantz and Guildenstern, two childhood friends of Hamlet, sent for by the King and Queen to probe the cause of Hamlet's madness.

King I entreat you both
That, being of so young days brought up with him,
And since so neighboured to[21] his youth and haviour,[22]
That you vouchsafe your rest here in our court
Some little time, so by your companies
To draw him on to pleasures and to gather,
So much as from occasion you may glean,
Whether aught to us unknown afflicts him thus
That, opened,[23] lies within our remedy.

We have already witnessed Claudius, Hamlet, and Polonius using false fronts to conceal the truth. Now Guildenstern and Rosencrantz are being instructed to do likewise: They are to spy on Hamlet under the cloak of friendship. There will be more deceptions to come, for the play is full of characters being false to one another because they fail to be true to themselves in the first place.

After the Queen thanks Rosencrantz and Guildenstern for coming, they respond thus:

Rosencrantz Both your Majesties
Might, by the sovereign power you have of us,
Put your dread pleasures more into command
Than to entreaty.

Guildenstern But we both obey,
And here give up ourselves in the full bent[24]
To lay our service freely at your feet
To be commanded.

---

21 **neighboured to** closely familiar with

22 **haviour** manners, behavior

23 **opened** revealed

24 **bent** extent

King Thanks, Rosencrantz and gentle Guildenstern.

Queen Thanks, Guildenstern and gentle Rosencrantz.

Rosencrantz and Guildenstern are strikingly indistinguishable. Guildenstern completes Rosencrantz's sentence for him; the King and Queen address them in complementary symmetrical sentences. Rosencrantz and Guildenstern function like Tweedledum and Tweedledee—we cannot tell them apart. What is Shakespeare's point? And why are there two of them, when, in fact, one character would have sufficed?

Rosencrantz and Guildenstern actually depict the bulk of us who are, in a sense, also indistinguishable. They represent the career-minded masses devoted to worldly ambition. With this mindset, we avoid the profound by selling our lives for material benefits, and end up like robots programmed to fulfill the dictates of our career. It is thus fitting for Guildenstern—on behalf of Rosencrantz as well—to say "we both obey, and here give up ourselves in the full bent to lay our service freely at your feet to be commanded." It is little wonder they are identical.

After the Queen dispatches them to seek out Hamlet, Polonius arrives. He informs Claudius that he has found the cause of Hamlet's lunacy. The King tells the Queen and elicits a very level-headed response:

King He tells me, my dear Gertrude, he hath found
The head and source of all your son's distemper.

Queen I doubt[25] it is no other but the main,[26]
His father's death and our o'er-hasty marriage.

Now, Voltemand and Cornelius, the ambassadors from Norway, enter and inform them that the King of Norway has reprimanded Fortinbras for preparing to wage war against Denmark without his knowledge. Voltemand then describes the response of Fortinbras:

Voltemand ...he, in brief, obeys
Receives rebuke from Norway, and, in fine,[27]
Makes vow before his uncle never more

---

25 **doubt** suspect

26 **main** main cause

27 **in fine** finally

To give th'assay[28] of arms against your Majesty.
Whereon old Norway, overcome with joy,
Gives him three thousand crowns in annual fee
And his commission to employ those soldiers
So levied, as before, against the Polack.

Fortinbras has acceded to the wishes of the King and is now preparing for a campaign against the Poles instead of confronting Denmark. He has given up waging war on the nation responsible for his father's death. Thus, among those with a father killed, one has not chosen the path of revenge. Ironically, Fortinbras, the one who forsakes vengeance, inherits the throne of Denmark in the end.

Meanwhile, happy with the outcome of this affair with Norway, the King turns his attention to Polonius who first indulges in an unnecessarily tedious prelude:

Polonius My liege and madam, to expostulate[29]
What majesty should be, what duty is,
Why day is day, night night, and time is time,
Were nothing but to waste night, day, and time.
Therefore, since brevity is the soul of wit,
And tediousness the limbs and outward flourishes,
I will be brief. Your noble son is mad.
Mad call I it, for to define true madness,
What is't but to be nothing else but mad?
But let that go.

Polonius's definition of madness as "nothing else but mad" is simplistic nonsense. Since Hamlet is deliberately putting on an "antic disposition," the statement actually emphasizes that madness is anything but easy to define. Also, in light of our steadfast refusal to accept the truth, all of us may be considered mad to some extent.

Of course, Polonius is more concerned with embellishing his speech than actually talking sense and the Queen's response draws our attention again to the motif of falsely beautifying things.

---

28 **assay** trial

29 **expostulate** discuss

Queen More matter with less art.

The Queen's response to Polonius's meaningless beautification of his own words is most apt, but it hardly curtails him:

Polonius Madam, I swear I use no art at all.
That he is mad 'tis true; 'tis true 'tis pity;
And pity 'tis 'tis true. A foolish figure![30]
But farewell it, for I will use no art.
Mad let us grant him then. And now remains
That we find out the cause of this effect,
Or rather say the cause of this defect,
For this effect defective comes by cause:
Thus it remains; and the remainder thus:

Finally, after all this, Polonius comes to the point.

Polonius Perpend,[31]
I have a daughter—have whilst she is mine—
Who in her duty and obedience, mark,
Hath given me this. Now gather and surmise.
[*Reads*] *To the celestial and my soul's idol, the most beautified Ophelia*—That's an ill phrase, a vile phrase, 'beautified' is a vile phrase. But you shall hear thus:
In her excellent white, bosom, these, etc.

The comment by Polonius that "'beautified' is a vile phrase" unexpectedly interrupts the flow of the action, and its incongruity draws our attention to it. This is exactly as Shakespeare intends for exactly the same reason as the interruption in Act I caused by Hamlet's sudden need to write down his observation that "one may smile, and smile, and be a villain." Both allude to our propensity to artificially beautify reality to conceal the truth, and there is a thematic resonance on this propensity throughout the play. The irony, here with Polonius, is that while he complains about the "vile phrase," he has himself presented a "beautified" speech, devoid of substance, before coming to the point.

---

30 **figure** figure of speech

31 **perpend** consider

Queen Came this from Hamlet to her?

Polonius Good madam, stay a while, I will be faithful.
Doubt that the stars are fire,
Doubt that the sun doth move,
Doubt truth to be a liar,
But never doubt I love.
Oh dear Ophelia, I am ill at these numbers.[32] *I have not art to reckon my groans. But that I love thee best, oh, most best, believe it. Adieu. Thine evermore, most dear lady, whilst this machine*[33] *is to him, Hamlet.*
This in obedience hath my daughter shown me,
And, more above,[34] hath his solicitings,
As they fell out by time, by means, and place,
All given to mine ear.

If Ophelia repelled Hamlet's letters following her father's command, this letter must have been written before Hamlet's feigned madness and hence is a genuine love article. Ophelia has betrayed Hamlet's trust in allowing the letter to be openly scrutinized.

Polonius now informs the King and Queen of his instructions for Ophelia to reject Hamlet's romantic advances. He claims Ophelia's obedience has led to Hamlet's madness. The King, however, having cause to be wary of Hamlet, has his doubts.

King Do you think 'tis this?

Queen It may be; very like.

Polonius Hath there been such a time—I would fain know that—
That I have positively said ''Tis so,'
When it proved otherwise?

King Not that I know.

Polonius Take this from this if this be otherwise
[*Points to his head and shoulder*]

---

32 **ill at these numbers** bad at making verses

33 **machine** body

34 **more above** furthermore

Polonius's assertion of confidence is amusing because we know he is wrong. The King, in any case, remains unconvinced and wants further proof:

King	How may we try it further?
Polonius	You know sometimes he walks four hours together Here in the lobby.
Queen	So he does indeed.
Polonius	At such a time I'll loose my daughter to him. Be you and I behind an arras[35] then. Mark the encounter: if he love her not, And be not from his reason fall'n thereon, Let me be no assistant for a state, But keep a farm and carters.
King	We will try it.

Thus the plans leading to the famous nunnery scene is laid. It is a plot for yet another act of being false to others, but this time, it involves the King, Queen, Polonius, and even Ophelia. All are guilty of not being true to themselves by steadfastly refusing to acknowledge the profound and the truth of their own mortality.

Now Hamlet wanders in, reading. Having requested the King and Queen to leave them alone together, Polonius addresses him. While Polonius intends to ferret out evidence for his theory of Hamlet's madness, Hamlet, knowing Polonius well, proceeds to toy with him. We thus have a comical display of the two being blatantly false to each other.

Nonetheless, the wild dialogue that ensues does provide a kaleidoscopic view of Hamlet's state of mind. It is akin to a psychological examination in which the patient rambles on through the use of free associations. We see in Hamlet a glimpse of a mind that faces the truth without beautification, but it is also a mind marred by vengeance and the condemnation of others.

Noticeably, Hamlet's words continually revolve around images of death. While saints and bodhisattvas of the past have stressed the importance of accepting our own mortality, they have, out of compassion,

---

[35] **arras** hanging tapestry

presented the concept gently and cautiously. Hamlet, however, is already being transformed by the poison of revenge and condemnation. He is not in the mood to be gentle, so when he talks about death, he taunts. Through Hamlet, Shakespeare subjects us to a form of shock treatment, one designed to shake us out of our complacency and our denial of the profound. This shock treatment becomes even more marked later in the play as the program of learning gradually intensifies.

Polonius Do you know me, my lord?

Hamlet Excellent well. You are a fishmonger.

This shattering discrepancy evokes laughter, but it is an appropriately sharp retort to the pompousness of Polonius.

Polonius Not I, my lord.

Hamlet Then I would you were so honest a man.

The motif of a lack of honesty recurs again. It can be interpreted at many levels, but the crucial one is our lack of honesty in facing reality.

Polonius Honest, my lord?

Hamlet Ay, sir. To be honest, as this world goes, is to be one man picked out of ten thousand.

Polonius That's very true, my lord.

The cynicism in Hamlet is evident. He has vowed to focus on vengeance and has added this to his bitterness over his mother's hasty remarriage. We are now witnessing its effect on him.

Hamlet For if the sun breed maggots in a dead dog, being a good kissing carrion[36]—Have you a daughter?

Polonius I have, my lord.

Hamlet Let her not walk i'th'sun. Conception[37] is a blessing, but as your daughter may conceive—friend, look to't.

Polonius [*Aside*] How say you by that? Still harping on my daughter.

---

36 **good kissing carrion** flesh good for kissing

37 **conception** understanding, or conceiving a child

Hamlet's statement on the breeding of maggots in a dead dog derives from the ancient idea that the sun creates new life from dead matter. He tells Polonius to keep his daughter away from the sun to prevent conception. However, following the pun between "sun" and "son," Hamlet is also obliquely hinting that he knows of Polonius's involvement in keeping his daughter away from him.

Polonius is not entirely wrong in thinking that Hamlet is affected by his daughter's rejection. To some extent, Hamlet's mind *is* preoccupied with his daughter. This is natural, but now it has taken on a bitterly cynical perspective.

Polonius	Yet he knew me not at first; he said I was a fishmonger. He is far gone. And truly in my youth I suffered much extremity for love, very near this. I'll speak to him again. What do you read, my lord?
Hamlet	Words, words, words.
Polonius	What is the matter, my lord?
Hamlet	Between who?
Polonius	I mean the matter that you read, my lord.
Hamlet	Slanders, sir. For the satirical rogue says here that old men have grey beards, that their faces are wrinkled, their eyes purging thick amber and plumtree gum, and that they have plentiful lack of wit, together with most weak hams—all which, sir, though I most powerfully and potently believe, yet I hold it not honesty to have it thus set down. For you yourself, sir, shall grow old as I am—if like a crab you could go backward.

This speech reminds us of an inevitable truth of life: We will all age and become what Hamlet has described. There is a curious play with words here in the form of a double reversal in Hamlet's statement. Although he says that it is "not honesty to have it thus set down," Hamlet actually means the opposite, i.e., that it is an honest statement (we may not like it, but the statement is clearly true). That he is reversing his words here is suggested by his next statement, which also reverses its meaning in stating that Polonius will grow as old as him.

Polonius [*Aside*] Though this be madness, yet there is method in't. Will you walk out of the air, my lord?

Hamlet Into my grave?

Polonius Indeed, that's out of the air. [*Aside*] How pregnant sometimes his replies are—a happiness that often madness hits on, which reason and sanity could not so prosperously be delivered of. I will leave him and suddenly contrive the means of meeting between him and my daughter. My lord, I will take my leave of you.

Hamlet You cannot, sir, take from me anything that I will not more willingly part withal—except my life, except my life, except my life.

Although he is deliberately toying with Polonius, Hamlet's words do provide a glimpse of his state of mind, which is bleak, cynical, and cluttered with images of death and decay.

Polonius Fare you well, my lord.

Hamlet These tedious old fools!

In the end, Hamlet directly voices his growing bitterness and cynicism. Polonius, however, is no wiser after having been manipulated by Hamlet. He remains convinced that Hamlet's madness is the result of Ophelia's rejection.

Rosencrantz and Guildenstern now arrive, and the exhibition of being false to one another continues with different participants. Although Hamlet is not entirely false initially, his attitude towards them deteriorates badly once he discerns their insincerity. This whole long dialogue between Hamlet and his childhood friends adds to the thematic resonance on deception and counter-deception that relentlessly intensifies throughout the play.

In his witty sallies, we gain more glimpses of Hamlet's mind:

Hamlet My excellent good friends. How dost thou, Guildenstern? Ah, Rosencrantz. Good lads, how do you both?

Rosencrantz As the indifferent[38] children of the earth.

Guildenstern Happy in that we are not over-happy: on Fortune's cap we are not the very button.

Hamlet Nor the soles of her shoe?

Rosencrantz Neither, my lord.

Hamlet Then you live about her waist, or in the middle of her favours?

Guildenstern Faith, her privates we.

Hamlet In the secret parts of Fortune? Oh most true, she is a strumpet.

Even Hamlet's bawdy remarks reflect his state of mind. He calls Fortune a whore. Further evidence of his cynicism follows:

Hamlet What news?

Rosencrantz None, my lord, but the world's grown honest.

Hamlet Then is doomsday near.

While this may be a general comment on man's basic lack of honesty, it particularly touches on the dishonesty with our own mortality, suggesting that it will be close to our doomsday before we acknowledge the reality of death.

Hamlet But your news is not true. Let me question more in particular. What have you, my good friends, deserved at the hands of Fortune that she sends you to prison hither?

Guildenstern Prison, my lord?

Hamlet Denmark's a prison.

Rosencrantz Then is the world one.

Hamlet A goodly one, in which there are many confines, wards,[39] and dungeons, Denmark being one o'th'worst.

---

38 **indifferent** ordinary

39 **wards** cells

Rosencrantz	We think not so, my lord.
Hamlet	Why, then 'tis none to you; for there is nothing either good or bad but thinking makes it so. To me, it is a prison.

To Hamlet, the world has become a prison, dark and pestilent. Why? Hamlet has steadfastly confronted the truths of life and has realized the inevitability of ageing and death. Under better circumstances, this perception would have caused him to realize the futility of worldly goals and to seek out the spiritual path, a path of love and compassion to save all beings from suffering. Taking this path would have led to a process of transformation to higher and higher states of mind, leading to the realization of nonseparation and the profound bliss of spiritual unity and oneness. This path to enlightenment, in the words of the Buddha, would have the taste of freedom.

Unfortunately, Hamlet has instead transformed his mind to one that is bent on vengeance, a mind that condemns and focuses on inflicting harm to another. This is a mind of separation that contradicts the spiritual path. The combination of this with the realization of mortality is an unmitigated disaster. The world becomes fatalistic and oppressive; it feels like a trap with dark walls inexorably closing in. Effectively, Hamlet's world has indeed become a prison. As he puts it, his thinking—or state of mind—makes it so.

The conversation now continues with the topic of ambition. This is not unexpected, since ambition is the lifeblood of these career men, Rosencrantz and Guildenstern.

Rosencrantz	Why, then your ambition makes it one: 'tis too narrow for your mind.

Rosencrantz, in line with the King's wishes, is fishing for information and hints that it is Hamlet's frustrated ambition to become king that makes his world a prison. However, Hamlet's perspective on life is already on a level above the mundane considerations of worldly ambition. What follows is a dialogue of double meanings with the two parties thinking along totally different lines.

Hamlet Oh, God, I could be bounded in a nutshell and count myself a king of infinite space—were it not that I have bad dreams.

Hamlet's prison, as he says, is caused by his state of mind, not by problems of ambition. Rosencrantz and Guildenstern, however, cannot leave the topic of ambition.

Guildenstern Which dreams indeed are ambition; for the very substance of the ambitious is merely the shadow of a dream.

Guildenstern means that an ambitious dream precedes the fulfillment of it. In this sense, the act of giving the dream substance is like its shadow that follows it. Hamlet turns this on its head.

Hamlet A dream itself is but a shadow.

Rosencrantz Truly, and I hold ambition of so airy and light a quality that it is but a shadow's shadow.

Rosencrantz is saying that ambition, being so airy and light, can take flight and reach very high levels, perhaps too high for Hamlet. Hamlet again turns this on its head.

Hamlet Then are our beggars bodies, and our monarchs and outstretched heroes the beggars' shadows.

Following their line of thought, Hamlet argues, it must then be concluded that it is the beggars who are substantial, and the ambitious ones—like monarchs and outstretched heroes—who are their shadows and hence inferior. It is a witty and appropriate retort.

Hamlet Shall we to th' court? For by my fay,[40] I cannot reason.

Both We'll wait upon you.

Hamlet No such matter. I will not sort you with the rest of my servants; for, to speak to you like an honest man, I am most dreadfully attended. But in the beaten way of friendship, what make you at Elsinore?

Rosencrantz To visit you, my lord, no other occasion.

---

40 **fay** faith

Hamlet Beggar that I am, I am even poor in thanks, but I thank you. And sure, dear friends, my thanks are too dear a halfpenny.[41] Were you not sent for? Is it your own inclining? Is it a free visitation?

When we read the play instead of watching it on stage, we may not realize that a pause now follows Hamlet's question as Rosencrantz and Guildenstern hesitate. Hamlet then continues:

Hamlet Come, come, deal justly with me.

Rosencrantz and Guildenstern still hesitate. This is the fateful turning point in Hamlet's relationship with his two childhood friends. By now, Hamlet already knows the answer to his question.

Hamlet Come, come. Nay, speak.

Guildenstern What should we say, my lord?

Hamlet Why, anything. But to the purpose. You were sent for, and there is a kind of confession in your looks, which your modesties have not craft enough to colour. I know the King and Queen have sent for you.

Rosencrantz To what end, my lord?

Hamlet That, you must teach me. But let me conjure you, by the rights of our fellowship, by the consonancy[42] of our youth, by the obligation of our ever-preserved love, and by what more dear a better proposer can charge you withal, be even and direct with me whether you were sent for or no.

Rosencrantz [*Aside to Guildenstern*] What say you?

Hamlet Nay, then I have an eye of you. If you love me, hold not off.

Guildenstern My lord, we were sent for.

The admission finally comes, but it is too late. From this time on, Hamlet no longer considers them his friends.

---

41 **too dear a halfpenny** not worth a halfpenny

42 **consonancy** harmonious companionship

Hamlet I will tell you why; so shall my anticipation prevent your discovery,[43] and your secrecy to the King and Queen moult no feather.[44] I have of late, but wherefore I know not, lost all my mirth, forgone all custom of exercises; and indeed it goes so heavily with my disposition that this goodly frame, the earth, seems to me a sterile promontory, this most excellent canopy the air, look you, this brave o'erhanging firmament, this majestical roof fretted[45] with golden fire, why, it appeareth nothing to me but a foul and pestilent congregation of vapours.

This speech echoes Hamlet's earlier statement that the world is a prison to him. Although Hamlet conceals his reason for feeling this way from Rosencrantz and Guildenstern, the description above reflects his state of mind—one brought on by the focus on condemnation and revenge. He continues in the same vein on his disposition toward the nature of man:

Hamlet What a piece of work is a man, how noble in reason, how infinite in faculties, in form and moving how express and admirable, in action how like an angel, in apprehension how like a god: the beauty of the world, the paragon of animals—and yet, to me, what is this quintessence of dust?

In describing man as "this quintessence of dust," Hamlet refers to man's mortality, something he is acutely aware of. The phrase, however, also suggests an inner mystical quality underlying man's limited existence on the mundane plane. It is, in fact, the aim of the spiritual quest to discover this quintessential quality and to bring it forth.

Hamlet Man delights not me—no, nor woman neither, though by your smiling you seem to say so.

Rosencrantz My lord, there was no such stuff in my thoughts.

Hamlet Why did ye laugh then, when I said man delights not me?

---

43 **prevent your discovery** forestall your disclosure

44 **moult no feather** remain intact, look unspoiled

45 **fretted** adorned, patterned as in fretwork

Rosencrantz To think, my lord, if you delight not in man, what lenten[46] entertainment the players shall receive from you. We coted[47] them on the way, and hither are they coming to offer you service.

Thus, we are introduced to the actors, later used by Hamlet to re-enact the murder of his father. Hamlet's interest in them is evident:

Hamlet He that plays the king shall be welcome—his majesty shall have tribute of me; the adventurous knight shall use his foil and target;[48] the lover shall not sigh gratis;[49] the humorous man shall end his part in peace; the clown shall make those laugh whose lungs are tickle o'th' sear;[50] and the lady shall say her mind freely, or the blank verse shall halt[51] for't. What players are they?

Rosencrantz Even those you were wont to take delight in; the tragedians of the city.

Hamlet How chances it they travel? Their residence, both in reputation and profit, was better both ways.

Rosencrantz I think their inhibition[52] comes by the means of the late innovation.

Hamlet Do they hold the same estimation they did when I was in the city? Are they so followed?

Rosencrantz No, indeed, they are not.

Hamlet How comes it? Do they grow rusty?

---

46 **lenten** meager

47 **coted** passed, overtook

48 **target** shield

49 **gratis** without reward

50 **tickle o'th' sear** easily triggered (the sear is the part of a gun that holds the hammer in position until released by the trigger)

51 **halt** limp

52 **inhibition** hindrance

Rosencrantz Nay, their endeavour keeps in the wonted pace, but there is, sir, an eyrie[53] of children, little eyases, that cry out on the top of question,[54] and are most tyrannically[55] clapped for't. These are now the fashion, and so berattle the common stages—so they call them—that many wearing rapiers are afraid of goose-quills[56] and dare scarce come thither.

The usurpation of the serious performers by the "little eyases" appropriately symbolizes our preference for trivial distractions rather than the real issues of life—an analogy Shakespeare uses to build on its thematic resonance. The mature players who portray reality are being driven out by the troupe of child-actors who mock them. A situation like this did actually arise in England during Shakespeare's time, and he obviously found it an apt analogy for our tendency to avoid the profound and hide behind distractions.

Hamlet What, are they children? Who maintains 'em? How are they escorted?[57] Will they pursue the quality[58] no longer than they can sing? Will they not say afterwards, if they should grow themselves to common players—as it is most like, if their means are no better—their writers do them wrong to make them exclaim against their own succession?[59]

Now the analogy becomes even more accurate. The child actors are deluding themselves and will face the consequences in time. Likewise, we will inevitably meet the profound whether or not we hide from it. Shakespeare stresses this idea by having virtually all the main characters die in the end. We cannot escape truth by indulging in distractions; we just end up facing it tragically unprepared.

---

53 **eyrie** nest

54 **cry out on the top of question** cry shrilly above others in the debate

55 **tyrannically** outrageously

56 **goose-quills** pens

57 **escorted** supported

58 **pursue the quality** continue their profession

59 **succession** future, what they will succeed to

Rosencrantz Faith, there has been much to do on both sides; and the nation holds it no sin to tar[60] them to controversy. There was for a while no money bid for argument unless the poet and the player went to cuffs in the question.

Hamlet Is't possible?

Guildenstern Oh, there has been much throwing about of brains.

Hamlet Do the boys carry it away?

Rosencrantz Ay, that they do, my lord; Hercules and his load too.

The world is the mythical load of Hercules. Shakespeare thus implies that the analogy concerning the child actors—depicting our propensity to indulge in distractions rather than face reality—applies to the whole world.

Hamlet It is not very strange; for my uncle is King of Denmark, and those that would make mouths at him while my father lived give twenty, forty, fifty, a hundred ducats apiece for his picture in little. 'Sblood, there is something in this more than natural, if philosophy could find it out.

There is indeed something unnatural in not facing the truth. We, like the masses in Denmark, will pay large sums for trivialities because they are the in-vogue distraction of the day, and yet we give no thought to the reality confronting us. Are we not mad? Truly, as Hamlet puts it, "there is something in this more than natural, if philosophy could find it out."

A flourish of trumpets now announces the arrival of the performers.

Guildenstern There are the players.

Hamlet Gentlemen, you are welcome to Elsinore. Your hands, come then. The appurtenance of welcome is fashion and ceremony. Let me comply with you in this garb—lest my extent to the players, which I tell you must show fairly outwards, should more appear like entertainment than yours. You are welcome.

---

60 **tar** incite

This show of cool formality to his two childhood friends is Hamlet's ironic way of announcing that he now merely considers them acquaintances. He no longer trusts them as friends and now considers them his enemies, spying on the King's behalf.

In his contrived act of formality, Hamlet also turns the tables of falsehood back onto Rosencrantz and Guildenstern. He is now as false to them as they were to him. The difference is that Hamlet scarcely conceals it.

Hamlet	But my uncle-father and aunt-mother are deceived.
Guildenstern	In what, my dear lord?
Hamlet	I am but mad north-north-west. When the wind is southerly, I know a hawk from a handsaw.

Now Hamlet toys with his former friends. While claiming that he is only slightly mad (i.e., only slightly off north), he asserts that at times, he can clearly distinguish a hawk from a handsaw, two items that bear absolutely no points for comparison. The statement suggests he is crazy, since even a madman can tell these two items apart.

However, typical of Hamlet's enigmatic statements, there is yet another meaning: If being north is being true, a southerly wind suggests treachery in the air. And since a hawk is a bird of prey, he may be issuing a subtle warning that, at such times, he can sniff out one.

Polonius now enters, and Hamlet immediately subjects him to cynical gibes, perhaps to illustrate the truth of the warning above:

Polonius	Well be with you, gentlemen.
Hamlet	Hark you, Guildenstern, and you too—at each ear a hearer. That great baby you see there is not yet out of his swaddling-clouts.
Rosencrantz	Happily he's the second time come to them, for they say an old man is twice a child.

Polonius's old age may account for his loss of astuteness, and we can sympathize. But not Hamlet—his cynicism has gone way beyond that.

Hamlet	I will prophesy he comes to tell me of the players. Mark it. You say right, sir, a Monday morning, 'twas then indeed.

Since his two childhood friends are spies, Hamlet probably realizes that Polonius, with his penchant for petty intrigues, would have been party to the arrangement. Now, by predicting Polonius's next action and pretending to be in conversation while observing him, Hamlet is turning the tables on Polonius. In a mocking way, Polonius has now become the one subjected to hidden scrutiny.

Polonius	My lord, I have news to tell you.
Hamlet	My lord, I have news to tell you. When Roscius[61] was an actor in Rome—
Polonius	The actors are come hither, my lord.
Hamlet	Buzz, buzz.
Polonius	Upon my honour—
Hamlet	Then came each actor on his ass—
Polonius	The best actors in the world, either for tragedy, comedy, history, pastoral, pastoral-comical, historical-pastoral, tragical-historical, tragical-comical-historical-pastoral, scene individable, or poem unlimited. Seneca[62] cannot be too heavy, nor Plautus[63] too light. For the law of writ, and the liberty, these are the only men.

Polonius's description of the performers is a parody of stuffy intellectualism. Hamlet breaks in with another of his enigmatic statements:

Hamlet	Oh, Jephthah, judge of Israel, what a treasure hadst thou!

Jephthah is a biblical character who, in exchange for victory in a battle, made a vow to kill the first person to greet him from his house. That first person turned out to be his only daughter, whom he eventually sacrificed after first allowing her time in the mountains to "bewail her virginity."

Polonius	What a treasure had he, my lord?

---

61 **Roscius** the most famous of Roman actors

62 **Seneca** Roman writer of tragedies

63 **Plautus** Roman writer of comedies

Hamlet Why,
'One fair daughter and no more,
The which he loved passing well.'

Polonius [*Aside*] Still on my daughter.

Hamlet actually quotes the lines from a ballad: "I read that many years ago,/When Jepha Judge of Israel,/Had one fair daughter and no more,/Whom he loved so passing well,/And as by lot God wot,/It came to pass most like it was…" Polonius's observation, however, is not entirely wrong. His presence does seem to remind Hamlet of his daughter, suggesting that Ophelia and her behavior, have seriously affected him.

Hamlet Am I not i'th'right, old Jephthah?

Polonius If you call me Jephthah, my lord, I have a daughter that I love passing well.

Hamlet Nay, that follows not.

Polonius What follows then, my lord?

Hamlet Why,
'As by lot God wot,' And then you know,
'It came to pass, as most like it was.'

By quoting the ballad lines that do "follow," Hamlet deliberately misinterprets Polonius and toys with him. Nonetheless, there is still the oblique hint that Polonius may be, in some way, sacrificing his daughter, a virgin, just as the biblical Jephthah did.

The players now enter to the warm welcome of Hamlet. He requests a performance of a passionate speech from a play he remembers:

Hamlet One speech in it I chiefly loved; 'twas Aeneas' tale to Dido; and thereabout of it especially when he speaks of Priam's slaughter. If it live in your memory, begin at this line—let me see, let me see—
The rugged Pyrrhus, like th'Hyrcanian beast—
It is not so. It begins with Pyrrhus—
The rugged Pyrrhus, he whose sable arms,

Black as his purpose, did the night resemble
When he lay couched in the ominous horse,[64]
Hath now this dread and black complexion smear'd
With heraldry more dismal. Head to foot
Now is he total gules, horridly tricked[65]
With blood of fathers, mothers, daughters, sons,
Baked and impasted[66] *with the parching streets,*
That lend a tyrannous and damned light
To their lord's murder. Roasted in wrath and fire,
And thus o'ersized with coagulate gore,
With eyes like carbuncles,[67] *the hellish Pyrrhus*
Old grandsire Priam seeks.
So proceed you.

Shakespeare presents us with a powerful and terrible imagery of the avenger. The avenger is Pyrrhus, whose father, Achilles, was killed in the Trojan War by Paris, the son of King Priam. Pyrrhus is now crouched in darkness within the Trojan Horse, preparing to wreak havoc on Troy and to kill Priam. Significantly, it is Hamlet who recites the first part of the speech that describes Pyrrhus, thus strengthening the link between himself and the image of terror it portrays.

Hamlet's false start provides us with the image of the Hyrcanian beast, which is a tiger, a predatory creature, colored black and red. These primitive hues are then intensified by the heraldic terms for black (sable) and red (gules) and used to suggest the darkness and flames of hell. Pyrrhus, "roasted in wrath and fire, and thus o'ersized with coagulate gore, with eyes like carbuncles," is thus depicted as a messenger from hell.

Shakespeare's intent is clear. As with the scene of the swearing ritual, he provides an experience of the diabolical and horrific nature of revenge.

The traveling actor now takes over from Hamlet:

1st Player *Anon he finds him,*
Striking too short at Greeks. His antique sword,
Rebellious to his arm, lies where it falls,

---

64 **ominous horse** the wooden Trojan horse

65 **tricked** decorated

66 **impasted** encrusted

67 **carbuncles** jewels believed to shine in the dark

Repugnant to command. Unequal matched,
Pyrrhus at Priam drives, in rage strikes wide;
But with the whiff and wind of his fell sword
Th'unnerved father falls. Then senseless Ilium,[68]
Seeming to feel this blow, with flaming top
Stoops to his base,[69] *and with a hideous crash*
Takes prisoner Pyrrhus' ear. For lo, his sword,
Which was declining on the milky head
Of reverend Priam, seemed i'th'air to stick;
So, as a painted tyrant, Pyrrhus stood,
And like a neutral to his will and matter,
Did nothing.
But as we often see against some storm
A silence in the heavens, the rack[70] *stand still,*
The bold winds speechless, and the orb below
As hush as death,...

With this dramatic pause, this haunting image of horror is frozen to linger in our minds. The avenger is poised like a demoniac monster ready to slaughter the helpless, while civilization collapses around him, giving way to his terrible will to soak all in blood and pain. After the pause, the avenger proceeds remorselessly with his brutal task:

1st Player *...anon the dreadful thunder*
Doth rend the region; so after Pyrrhus' pause
Aroused vengeance sets him new awork,
And never did the Cyclops' hammers fall
On Mar's armour, forged for proof eterne,[71]
With less remorse than Pyrrhus' bleeding sword
Now falls on Priam.
Out, out, thou strumpet Fortune! All you gods
In general synod[72] *take away her power,*

68 **Ilium** the citadel of Troy

69 **stoops to his base** collapses

70 **rack** cloud formations

71 **proof eterne** eternal endurance

72 **synod** council

	Break all the spokes and fellies[73] *from her wheel,* *And bowl the round nave*[74] *down the hill of heaven* *As low as to the fiends.*
Polonius	This is too long.
Hamlet	It shall to the barber's with your beard! Prithee say on. He's for a jig or a tale of bawdry, or he sleeps. Say on, come to Hecuba.

Hamlet has several scenes that seem unnecessary to the action of the play. Nonetheless, Shakespeare includes them because they are focused allegorical scenes deliberately crafted to artistically amplify the meaning of the play. In fact, these scenes now serve as the best clues to Shakespeare's intended meaning—if they do not contribute to its action, they contribute to its message.

Scenes of this nature include the long swearing ritual in Act I, the dialogue between Polonius and Reynaldo in Act II, Hamlet's instructions to the players in Act III, the campaign of Fortinbras against Poland in Act IV, the long conversations between Hamlet and the gravedigger and between Hamlet and Osric in Act V, and, of course, this long speech on Pyrrhus's slaughter of Priam.

Polonius's remark that the speech is "too long" may then be Shakespeare's anticipation of his critics' response. It enables him to answer his critics directly by Hamlet's reply. From it, we know Shakespeare is aware the speech on Pyrrhus is long. Also, we know by his insistence on continuing with it, that it is relevant to the play.

The speech is Shakespeare's commentary on the horror of revenge. Note that it is with "aroused vengeance" that Pyrrhus resumed his bloody task after the pause. The player continues:

1st Player	*But who—ah, woe!—had seen the mobbled*[75] *queen—*
Hamlet	'The mobbled queen'?
Polonius	That's good.

---

73 **fellies** rims

74 **nave** hub

75 **mobbled** muffled

1st Player *Run barefoot up and down, threat'ning the flames*
With bisson rheum,[76] *a clout*[77] *upon that head*
Where late the diadem stood, and, for a robe,
About her lank and all o'erteemed[78] *loins*
A blanket, in th'alarm of fear caught up—
Who this had seen, with tongue in venom steeped,
'Gainst Fortune's state would treason have pronounced.
But if the gods themselves did see her then,
When she saw Pyrrhus make malicious sport,
In mincing with his sword her husband's limbs,
The instant burst of clamour that she made,
Unless things mortal move them not at all,
Would have made milch[79] *the burning eyes of heaven*
And passion in the gods.

The player's speech now focuses on the terrible toll vengeance exacts on the innocent. The intended targets of the avenger are not the only ones who suffer. Vengeance seldom stays confined but instead reverberates around with dreadful intensity, dragging many into its mesh of sorrow. This will also be the case with Hamlet's own quest for revenge.

Polonius Look whe'er he has not turned his colour and has tears in's eyes. Prithee no more.

The actor's emotional reaction ironically serves as a cue for Hamlet to chide himself for delaying his revenge.

Hamlet 'Tis well. I'll have thee speak out the rest of this soon. Good my lord, will you see the players well bestowed?[80] Do you hear, let them be well used, for they are the abstract and brief chronicles of the time. After your death you were better to have a bad epitaph than their ill report while you live.

---

76 **bisson rheum** blinding tears

77 **clout** cloth

78 **o'erteemed** worn out by childbearing

79 **milch** tearful (literally, milk-giving)

80 **bestowed** lodged

Polonius My lord, I will use them according to their desert.

Hamlet God's bodykins, man, much better. Use every man after his desert, and who shall scape whipping? Use them after your own honour and dignity: the less they deserve, the more merit is in your bounty.

Hamlet's statement is true—justice for all will land us in severe trouble. Interestingly, when we "demand justice," we are demanding either a reward for ourselves or punishment for others. It is never the reverse.

The real solution lies not in justice, but more in forgiveness, which is the act of compassion. Even if we want transgressors to learn from the consequences of their actions, we must seek to have them learn purely for their benefit. Punishment should never be meted out as revenge, and never with malicious intent.

Tragically, Hamlet fails to heed his own words and plunges onward to disaster. The players now prepare to leave with Polonius.

Hamlet Follow him, friends. We'll hear a play tomorrow. [*To 1st Player*] Dost thou hear me, old friend? Can you play The Murder of Gonzago?

1st Player Ay, my lord.

Hamlet We'll ha't tomorrow night. You could for a need study a speech of some dozen or sixteen lines, which I would set down and insert in't, could you not?

1st Player Ay, my lord.

Hamlet plans for the players to re-enact his father's murder in a scheme to expose Claudius's guilt. The cycle of deception and counter-deception continues unabated.

The players leave with Polonius, followed shortly by Rosencrantz and Guildenstern. Hamlet is finally alone, and the stage is set for the soliloquy that gave rise to one of the most persistent mysteries in literature: Why does Hamlet delay his revenge?

Hamlet Ay, so, God buy you. Now I am alone.
Oh, what a rogue and peasant slave am I!

Is it not monstrous that this player here,
But in a fiction, in a dream of passion,
Could force his soul so to his whole conceit[81]
That from her working all his visage wanned,
Tears in his eyes, distraction in his aspect,
A broken voice, and his whole function suiting
With forms to his conceit? And all for nothing!
For Hecuba!
What's Hecuba to him, or he to Hecuba,
That he should weep for her? What would he do
Had he the motive and the cue for passion
That I have? He would drown the stage with tears,
And cleave the general ear with horrid speech,
Make mad the guilty and appal the free,[82]
Confound the ignorant, and amaze indeed
The very faculties of eyes and ears.
Yet I,
A dull and muddy-mettled[83] rascal, peak
Like John-a-dreams,[84] unpregnant[85] of my cause,
And can say nothing—no, not for a king,
Upon whose property and most dear life
A damned defeat was made. Am I a coward?
Who calls me a villain, breaks my pate across,
Plucks off my beard and blows it in my face,
Tweaks me by the nose, gives me the lie i'th'throat
As deep as to the lungs? Who does me this?
Ha, 'swounds, I should take it; for it cannot be
But I am pigeon-livered and lack gall
To make oppression bitter, or ere this
I should ha'fatted all the region kites

---

81 **conceit** imagination

82 **free** innocent, free from guilt

83 **muddy-mettled** dull-spirited

84 **John-a-dreams** a dreaming person

85 **unpregnant** not quickened to action

With this slave's offal. Bloody, bawdy villain!
Remorseless, treacherous, lecherous, kindless villain!
Oh, vengeance!
Why, what an ass am I! This is most brave,
That I, the son of a dear father murdered,
Prompted to my revenge by heaven and hell,
Must like a whore unpack my heart with words
And fall a-cursing like a very drab,[86]
A scullion![87] Fie upon't! Foh!

This is Hamlet's first long soliloquy chiding himself for his delay in wreaking vengeance. The reason for the delay is of utmost importance because the meaning of the play revolves around it. It is therefore crucial to study it closely.

The reason for Hamlet's delay has haunted critics for four centuries. Different authors have presented differing reasons for the delay, which, in itself, raises another question concerning this puzzling aspect of the play: Why does Shakespeare give so much prominence to the delay without clearly presenting the reason for it? The answer helps point us toward Shakespeare's own reason for Hamlet's delay.

We must keep two things in mind. First, Shakespeare makes it clear that Hamlet is acutely aware of a delay. Second, Shakespeare also makes it clear that Hamlet himself is not sure why he delays. There is no need for Shakespeare to emphasize these two things unless he is making a point. What is that point?

Let us first look at some of the more prominent reasons on offer for Hamlet's delay. One solution claims that there is actually no delay on Hamlet's part, or that any delay is due to external difficulties. The truth is that we might not have noticed the delay if Hamlet himself had not brought it to our attention. Shakespeare stresses the point that Hamlet is delaying. Thus, it is meaningless to argue that Hamlet is not responsible for the delay when Shakespeare clearly wants us to see that he is.

In the eighteenth century, critics suggested that the delay is a necessary plot device to extend the action. However, this suggestion does not fit

86 **drab** prostitute

87 **scullion** the lowest of kitchen servants, noted for foul language

the facts, since there would then be no reason for Shakespeare to make the delay so conspicuous by having Hamlet bemoan it over two long soliloquies.

At the end of the eighteenth century, Goethe proposed that Shakespeare means, in Hamlet, to "represent the effects of a great action laid upon a soul unfit for the performance of it."[88] In his words, "A lovely, pure, noble and most moral nature, without the strength of nerve which forms a hero, sinks beneath a burden which it cannot bear and must not cast away." Thus Goethe painted the picture of a tender, sensitive youth who could not bring himself to perform the act of vengeance upon his uncle. However, even if Hamlet had this sweet nature before receiving the terrible mandate from the ghost, it hardly describes the transformed Hamlet we see in the play. We find instead a Hamlet who can be terrible and ruthless in his actions, well depicted in his callous taunting remarks after he accidentally kills Polonius and in his offhand manner when relating how he dispatches his former school friends to their untimely deaths. As A. C. Bradley puts it: "If the sentimental Hamlet had crossed him, he would have hurled him from his path with one sweep of the arm."

In the nineteenth century, the romantics A. W. Schlegel[89] and S. T. Coleridge[90] offered the solution that Hamlet is rendered incapable of action because of his tendency to philosophize too much. Taking the cue from his own words, they proposed that Hamlet's "native hue of resolution is sicklied o'er with the pale cast of thought." According to Coleridge, Hamlet had "great, enormous, intellectual activity, and a consequent proportionate aversion to real action." Coleridge concluded that "Shakespeare wished to impress upon us the truth that action is the chief end of existence."

The problem with this argument is that Laertes behaves in exactly the opposite way to Hamlet, and compared to Hamlet, Laertes fares even worse. Laertes virtually acts without forethought and becomes a naïve and willing tool of Claudius, the villain himself. Thus, to behave in this

---

88 From *Wilhelm Meister's Apprenticeship* by Johann Wolfgang von Goethe (1795), translated by Thomas Carlyle.

89 See *Lectures on Dramatic Art and Literature* by Augustus William Schlegel (1808), translated by John Black (London, 1846).

90 See *Coleridge's Shakespearean Criticism,* ed. Thomas M. Raysor (London: Constable, 1930).

manner can hardly be the message that Shakespeare wishes to impart. Also, the behavior of Hamlet in rushing headlong against all restraints to follow a beckoning ghost; in rashly running his rapier through Polonius hiding behind the arras; in boldly boarding the pirate ship in the sea battle; and in leaping into a grave to grapple with Laertes, hardly fits the description of one with an aversion to real action.

At the beginning of the twentieth century, A. C. Bradley proposed another reason for the delay in his *Shakespearean Tragedy*.[91] Bradley argued that Hamlet's delay is the result of a melancholic state of mind, brought on by the death of his father and the hasty remarriage of his mother. While we may accept that a depressive state of mind causes Hamlet's inaction, this idea becomes highly suspect when Bradley stated that Hamlet's melancholia accounts for his energy as well.

Hamlet certainly gives much evidence of energy in his sharp and witty sallies, in his obvious interest in the art of the traveling actors, in his dramatic recitation of the speech on Pyrrhus, in his clever arrangement of the play scene to trap Claudius, and in the way he engineered the demise of Rosencrantz and Guildenstern. These actions are hardly characteristic of depression. Also, most of these energetic actions are rationally motivated and some even carefully schemed out. If Hamlet is capable of carrying out such actions, he is certainly capable of exacting revenge on his uncle. So if Shakespeare intends melancholy to be the reason for Hamlet's delay, he certainly does a bad job of portraying it; furthermore, he really has no message at all to deliver in the play.

Another reason offered for Hamlet's delay was the psychoanalytical one, first suggested by Freud, the originator of psychoanalysis. According to this theory, Hamlet is rendered incapable of acting against Claudius because of a repressed Oedipus complex; he restrains his actions because he has a subconscious desire to replace his father and lie with his mother. However, a strong argument can be made against this proposal, for such an intent on Shakespeare's part would have been totally lost on the Elizabethan audience. They certainly did not have the benefit of Freud's theories to rely on, and it would have required Shakespeare to make this reason for the delay a lot clearer than he did. The fact that Shakespeare did not do so reinforces the argument against this proposal.

---

91 *Shakespearean Tragedy* by A. C. Bradley (Macmillan & Co., 1904).

In fact, it was because T. S. Eliot[92] agreed with a similar kind of psychoanalytical reason for Hamlet's delay that he called the play an "artistic failure," and Shakespeare would certainly seem to have failed miserably in this sense if this was his reason for Hamlet's delay. Given Shakespeare's artistic ability, it instead suggests that Eliot's famous remark actually argues against a psychoanalytical reason for the delay. Moreover, it is no help to say that Shakespeare may have subconsciously implanted the concept into the play, because it then becomes an invalid explanation for his clear intent to make the delay a prominent issue.

So what was Shakespeare's reason for having Hamlet so conspicuously chide himself for the delay and yet not understand why he was delaying? We have to come back to the one reason that would, at least, have occurred to the Elizabethan audience: that there was a question of immorality in seeking revenge. Herman Ulrici raised this issue in the nineteenth century, but critics neglected it largely because A. C. Bradley had argued so effectively against conscience being the reason for the delay.

Since Hamlet himself is not aware of the reason for the delay, it is not conscience taken in its usual form that we are considering. It is, instead, a more deep-seated inner voice that causes him to hesitate, a voice that Hamlet fails to bring explicitly to the surface of his consciousness. Bradley, however, also objected to this deeper conscience as the reason for the delay. Why, he asked, if this answers to Shakespeare's meaning, did he then conceal that meaning until the last Act? However, this objection becomes invalid once we fully understand Shakespeare's reason for the delay and why he highlighted it.

Shakespeare gives prominence to the delay because he wants to emphasize that Hamlet's course of action is morally dubious. Also, Shakespeare does not try to conceal this meaning until the end; he actually took great pains to suggest it, right from the beginning of the play. What he could not do, however, is to allow Hamlet to state it explicitly. There is a very good reason for not allowing this. If Hamlet had recognized the cause of his delay, it would have altered the course of the action and defeated Shakespeare's main purpose in the play.

---

92 See "Hamlet and His Problems" from *Selected Essays* by T. S. Eliot (Harcourt Brace Jovanovich, 1950).

Shakespeare's aim is not to have Hamlet intellectually argue out the question of whether or not it is immoral to wreak vengeance. His intention is to have the audience find the answer to this question in the experience of the entire play, in its totality. This is Shakespeare's method of conveying his message, and it is the most effective way to do so. Shakespeare makes us live through it so that we learn through our emotional involvement and our experience of it.

If Hamlet had recognized intellectually that a moral issue was causing his delay, he would certainly have argued it out with himself. It would have been completely out of character for him not to do so. But to have him conduct an intellectual debate on the issue would have totally defeated Shakespeare's purpose, which was to show and not merely tell, why seeking revenge is a moral disaster.

To do that, Shakespeare needs Hamlet to follow the course of action in the play. If Hamlet had debated the moral issue with himself, he would either conclude that it is morally acceptable, which would contradict what Shakespeare wanted to convey, or he would conclude that it is morally wrong and abandon his course of vengeance. Since neither alternative is conducive to Shakespeare's plan, he allows Hamlet to delay without explicitly debating the moral issue.

And so, Shakespeare has Hamlet make the same mistake that Brutus makes in *Julius Caesar*; this is the reason Julius Caesar is mentioned on three separate occasions in *Hamlet*. Like Brutus, Hamlet fails to align himself with the divine and does not flow with the Tao. Hamlet ignores his inner voice, his deep conscience telling him that his course of action is wrong, that seeking vengeance amounts to taking the dark path to moral destruction. His inner promptings do cause him to delay, but he does not recognize why, so he tragically follows the route to spiritual desecration. Now Shakespeare is able to achieve his purpose. By the dramatic portrayal of Hamlet's transformation along this terrible path of vengeance, Shakespeare forces his audience to experience why revenge is wrong.

Even at this stage of the play, Shakespeare has taken great pains to suggest that there is something deeply wrong with revenge. He reminds us many times that the ghost is not an enlightened being and that its counsel is suspect. He impresses upon us the diabolical nature of the ghost's mandate through the eerie swearing ritual at the end of Act I. He illustrates the effect of this mandate on Hamlet's mind—the transformation of his world into a sinister and dark prison. He also creates the experience of the horror of vengeance through the terrifying depiction of the avenger in the Trojan War speech.

Now, by placing Hamlet's self-criticism for his delay immediately after this recitation, Shakespeare again suggests that Hamlet has good reason to hesitate. In fact, the entire play serves to impress upon us the error of revenge. It demonstrates why revenge is wrong and makes us experience it. Thus, *Hamlet* is far from being an artistic failure; it is close to being an artistic miracle.

Let us now examine more closely Hamlet's first soliloquy on his delay. He begins by contrasting the passion of the player in his speech with his own lack of positive action and chides himself for it. There is much irony in this attitude. First, the performer is only acting. His passion is conjured up without any actual cause and is merely an outer image made to fit what is conventionally expected. Thus Hamlet is railing over mere appearance.

Also, the absence of a real motive for the actor's passion dramatically depicts that emotional fervor can arise in the absence of rational cause. This fact reminds us that the thirst for vengeance results mainly from passion, not reason. We know that revenge cannot undo the harm already inflicted and is actually far more likely to aggravate it. Hamlet himself ironically emphasizes this problem of irrational passion later: "Give me that man that is not passion's slave, and I will wear him in my heart's core, ay, in my heart of hearts…" It is the tragedy of Hamlet that he often does not heed his own wise words.

Another irony lies in the fact that the passion of the actor is that of compassion for Hecuba, whose suffering has been inflicted by none other than an avenger. Hamlet's self-reproach for his delay in seeking vengeance, therefore, is for a lack of what caused Hecuba's anguish in the first place. Thus, Hamlet uses a totally inappropriate cue for chiding himself over the delay. By this deep irony, Shakespeare hints at the immoral nature of revenge.

The soliloquy then continues with Hamlet wondering whether he is a coward for delaying his act of vengeance. From his manner of confronting the ghost and his reputation as a model soldier, we know, however, that

Hamlet does not lack courage. Thus, Shakespeare's aim here is to show that Hamlet himself is unsure why he delays.

The soliloquy now ends with the hint that Hamlet doubts whether taking revenge on his uncle is the proper course of action. Unfortunately and tragically, he only admits to doubts on the ghost's honesty, not to doubts on the morality of vengeance.

Hamlet About, my brains. I have heard
That guilty creatures sitting at a play
Have, by the very cunning of the scene,
Been struck so to the soul that presently
They have proclaimed their malefactions.
For murder, though it have no tongue, will speak
With most miraculous organ. I'll have these players
Play something like the murder of my father
Before mine uncle. I'll observe his looks;
I'll tent[93] him to the quick. If he but blench,[94]
I know my course. The spirit that I have seen
May be a devil, and the devil hath power
T'assume a pleasing shape, yea, and perhaps,
Out of my weakness and my melancholy,
As he is very potent with such spirits,
Abuses me to damn me. I'll have grounds
More relative[95] than this. The play's the thing
Wherein I'll catch the conscience of the King.

Hamlet thus prepares to spring his "mouse-trap" on the King. He follows the path of vengeance with disastrous consequences. Now we can experience for ourselves why revenge is wrong.

---

93 **tent** probe

94 **blench** flinch

95 **relative** closely related

3

Act III

Scene 1

In Act III, deceit and falsehood continue to swirl in ever-desperate circles. Scene 1 opens with the King, Queen, and Polonius in consultation with Rosencrantz and Guildenstern. Significantly, everyone here is now involved in being false to someone else; this may be ultimately attributed to not being true to themselves in the first place. Now the pattern of deceit takes on a strange reciprocal symmetry, a bizarre dance of deception and counter-deception.

King And can you by no drift of conference[1]
Get from him why he puts on this confusion,
Grating so harshly all his days of quiet
With turbulent and dangerous lunacy?

The falsehood of Rosencrantz and Guildenstern, spying under the cloak of renewing old friendship is met with the counter-deception of Hamlet's pretended madness.

Rosencrantz He does confess he feels himself distracted,
But from what cause he will by no means speak.

Guildenstern Nor do we find him forward[2] to be sounded,[3]
But with a crafty madness keeps aloof
When we would bring him on to some confession
Of his true state.

---

1 **drift of conference** steering of conversation

2 **forward** willing

3 **sounded** probed

The King's suspicion that Hamlet's antic disposition may be "put on" is further fuelled by Guildenstern's hint that his madness is not his "true state."

The pattern of deceit now continues with reference to the play designed by Hamlet to spy on the conscience of the King.

Queen Did you assay[4] him
To any pastime?

Rosencrantz Madam, it so fell out that certain players
We o'erraught[5] on the way. Of these we told him,
And there did seem in him a kind of joy
To hear of it. They are here about the court,
And, as I think, they have already order
This night to play before him.

Polonius 'Tis most true,
And he beseeched me to entreat your Majesties
To hear and see the matter.

King With all my heart; and it doth much content me
To hear him so inclined.
Good gentlemen, give him a further edge,[6]
And drive his purpose into these delights.

Ironically, the King is happy with the one action of Hamlet he has reason to fear—Hamlet's plan to spy on him in a contrived situation. And now, continuing the dance of deception and counter-deception, the King reciprocates by announcing his own plan to spy on Hamlet in another contrived situation.

King Sweet Gertrude, leave us too,
For we have closely[7] sent for Hamlet hither
That he, as 'twere by accident, may here
Affront[8] Ophelia.

---

4 **assay** tempt

5 **o'erraught** overtook

6 **edge** stimulus

7 **closely** privately

8 **affront** meet face to face

Her father and myself, lawful espials,[9]
Will so bestow ourselves that, seeing unseen,
We may of their encounter frankly judge,
And gather by him, as he is behaved,
If't be th'affliction of his love or no
That thus he suffers for.

Queen I shall obey you.
And for your part, Ophelia, I do wish
That your good beauties be the happy cause
Of Hamlet's wildness; so shall I hope your virtues
Will bring him to his wonted way again,
To both your honours.

Ophelia Madam, I wish it may.

Neither the Queen nor Ophelia shows any aversion to a romantic relationship between Hamlet and Ophelia. Thus, Polonius's advice for Ophelia to reject Hamlet's advances is unwarranted.

Polonius Ophelia, walk you here. Gracious, so please you,
We will bestow ourselves. Read on this book,
That show of such an exercise may colour
Your loneliness.[10] We are oft to blame in this,
'Tis too much proved, that with devotion's visage
And pious action we do sugar o'er
The devil himself.

King [*Aside*] Oh, 'tis too true.
How smart a lash that speech doth give my conscience!
The harlot's cheek, beautied with plast'ring art,
Is not more ugly to the thing that helps it
Than is my deed to my most painted word.
Oh heavy burden!

Again, we encounter the thematic resonance of something rotten being beautified to conceal its true character. Often, this lack of honesty also taints our perception of the world. Unable to face the profound, we blind

---

9 **espials** spies

10 **colour your loneliness** explain your being alone

ourselves to the truth and often consider what is bad as good. We falsely beautify what we see. The recurrence of this motif concerning the word "beautified" as the "vile phrase" is an apt prologue to what comes next in the play.

Polonius I hear him coming. Let's withdraw, my lord.

Hamlet now enters, and before encountering Ophelia, delivers the most famous and most celebrated monologue in English literature:

Hamlet To be, or not to be, that is the question:
Whether 'tis nobler in the mind to suffer
The slings and arrows of outrageous fortune,
Or to take arms against a sea of troubles
And by opposing end them. To die, to sleep—
No more; and by a sleep to say we end
The heart-ache and the thousand natural shocks
That flesh is heir to: 'tis a consummation
Devoutly to be wished. To die, to sleep;
To sleep, perchance to dream—ay, there's the rub: [11]
For in that sleep of death what dreams may come,
When we have shuffled off this mortal coil, [12]
Must give us pause—there's the respect
That makes calamity of so long life.
For who would bear the whips and scorns of time,
The oppressor's wrong, the proud man's contumely,
The pangs of despised love, the law's delay,
The insolence of office, and the spurns
That patient merit of the unworthy takes,
When he himself might his quietus [13] make
With a bare bodkin? [14] Who would fardels [15] bear,
To grunt and sweat under a weary life,
But that the dread of something after death,

---

11 **rub** obstacle

12 **coil** turmoil

13 **quietus** settlement

14 **bodkin** dagger

15 **fardels** burdens

The undiscovered country, from whose bourn [16]
No traveller returns, puzzles the will,
And make us rather bear those ills we have
Than fly to others that we know not of?
Thus conscience does make cowards of us all,
And thus the native hue of resolution
Is sicklied o'er with the pale cast of thought,
And enterprises of great pitch [17] and moment
With this regard their currents turn awry
And lose the name of action. Soft you now,
The fair Ophelia! Nymph, in thy orisons [18]
Be all my sins remembered.

This soliloquy is the pivotal point of the play. After the relative lull of Act II, it is the ominous calm before the storm. After it, the action returns with furious intensity, and Hamlet's apt closing line, "Be all my sins remembered," signals the unleashing of all the pent-up forces created by his vow of vengeance. This speech is probably also the most discussed in Shakespeare, and its meaning is crucial to the play. It delves into the stark reality of life and death with deep reverberations of meaning. What is Shakespeare trying to say?

Hamlet contemplates the nature of our existence, of life and death. These, we must realize, are not the usual reflections of an average person whose mind is instead often preoccupied with mundane distractions. We generally do not delve deeply into issues of this nature but rather avoid them because they are painful. In Hamlet, then, we see the deep contemplation of one who has courageously confronted the truth and faced the stark reality stripped of all the worldly clutter. He also strips away all the artificially beautified images we create of our worldly life in order to conceal what is rotten inside.

Hamlet thus sees the profound reality as the Buddha sees it: Our mundane existence is in the nature of suffering. Hence arises the question of whether it is not better to end our lives than to bear up with all the

16 **bourn** realm

17 **pitch** height (a term from falconry)

18 **orisons** prayers

"slings and arrows" of this mundane world. If this really is the true picture of life, and if inevitable death brings all our worldly achievements to naught, it would be reasonable to propose an early exit.

Yet something holds us back. To Hamlet, it is the uncertainty of what may happen beyond death. Some may take this to mean the fear of punishment for our transgressions, but a careful examination of the soliloquy shows that Shakespeare does not have Hamlet explicitly express that fear. All that is stated specifically is that the uncertainty of "what dreams may come" in the "sleep of death," or "the dread of something after death," gives us cause to hesitate.

Shakespeare, then, may well be alluding to something deeper, something more than the mere intellectual or doctrinal issue of punishment for transgressions. The soliloquy suggests that the meaning of life does not end at the worldly boundaries of our mundane existence. It lies in spiritual depths that transcend death and the temporary passage of our earthly life. If we are in contact with this profound depth within us, we will know that it is an error to flee the trials of life by suicide. Hamlet thus states that it is our conscience that makes us hesitate to take our own lives because, painful though it is, there is a reason for our being in this world. We must not run away by suicide because there is another solution to the sufferings of our mundane existence, and it is to learn this solution that is why we are here.

Hamlet's soliloquy also hints at the reason for his delay in taking revenge. After the statement, "Thus conscience does make cowards of us all," Hamlet follows up with the sentence: "And thus the native hue of resolution is sicklied o'er with the pale cast of thought." [19] The second "thus" in this sentence generalizes our restraint to actions other than suicide. These actions must surely include what is of great concern to Hamlet at this time: the act of revenge. The monologue thus hints

---

19 The proposal by Schlegel and Coleridge—that Hamlet's delay was due to his propensity to dwell too much in his thoughts—is derived partly from this statement. This reading of the statement, however, is an error in interpretation; it comes from looking at this sentence out of the context of the whole soliloquy. If it is Shakespeare's purpose to show that philosophizing too much hampers action and is thus a fault, as Coleridge suggests, it would follow in the context of the soliloquy that Hamlet should proceed with suicide and not think too much about it. Encouraging suicide would hardly be Shakespeare's intent.

that Hamlet's conscience is making him hesitate at both suicide and revenge.

Shakespeare again does not have Hamlet explicitly state why he delays his vengeance because if Hamlet acknowledges his conscience as the cause, he would be compelled to alter his course of action, and this would defeat Shakespeare's purpose to make us experience why revenge is wrong. Shakespeare, however, does suggest that conscience is the underlying factor by pointing to a connection between why we do not end our own lives and why Hamlet delays. The underlying reason for both is the same. If Hamlet really searches deep within, he will know that both suicide and revenge are wrong, just as we do. In the words of Lao Tzu, these actions amount to fighting against the Tao instead of flowing with it. Both suicide and revenge run against our deep conscience. Why?

The solution to the sufferings of our mundane existence lies in taking the spiritual path, a path of progressive realization of the higher spiritual truths. We must not run away from this task by suicide. We have to learn from the trials and tribulations of life and go through a purification of fire. And we must refrain from condemning others and from seeking vengeance because that is exactly what we have to learn to avoid. We are here to transform ourselves on the spiritual path that leads ultimately to the profound bliss of unity and oneness. Condemning others and seeking revenge will destroy this process because the spiritual path is a path to save all beings, without exception.

The reason Shakespeare suggests that both suicide and revenge are wrong should now be clear: We must not commit suicide because we are here to learn the solution to our suffering by taking the spiritual path, and we must not seek revenge because that would directly contradict the spiritual path.

Confronting the profound, facing the inevitability of death, and realizing the actual nature of our existence, are the first steps towards embarking on the spiritual quest. Hamlet takes these first steps. Proceeding correctly, they will provide the motivation and the drive to focus all our energies on the spiritual path to salvation. Tragically for Hamlet, however, he has been led astray and has taken instead a route to disaster. That route is the path of vengeance, which is in direct contradiction to the spiritual process. For the spiritual path is a path of the heart, a path of compassion and forgiveness, a path of giving and self-sacrifice, leading to the state of union and a sense of oneness with the all. Revenge mocks this path and substitutes a path of separation—a path of isolation from the all—that leads to spiritual desecration. It will lead to the living hell that Hamlet has described in Act II, transforming his whole world into a vile prison.

We can now understand the link between the two main themes in the play: the need to confront the truth, and the error of seeking revenge. We can view this from two complementary perspectives. In the first, *Hamlet* can be seen as a play that brings home to us the need to face the truth of life, as this is an essential step on the spiritual path. The play also illustrates the nature of this spiritual path, a path of love and compassion, and hence emphasizes that revenge, as well as the condemnation of others, has no place in it.

Viewing the play from the second perspective, *Hamlet* can be seen as drama designed to demonstrate the error of seeking vengeance, and more significantly, to make us experience why it is wrong. Revenge is wrong because there is only one route to salvation from the sufferings of our mundane existence, and this route is utterly destroyed by a mind focused on vengeance. Not only that, if we have already taken the first step in facing the profound, the path of vengeance becomes even more devastating for us and leads to a state of bitter cynicism and total desolation. The world then becomes an appalling dungeon, cold and futile.

The closing line of the soliloquy—"be all my sins remembered"—reminds us that Hamlet has yet to take the spiritual path, which means that neither suicide nor seeking vengeance is proper. Significantly, this closing line of the soliloquy is stated in the context of Hamlet asking Ophelia to remember his sins in her prayers. This, in effect, is a request for compassion.

Hamlet, unfortunately, is already caught up in the dark tide of vengeance, and we see its effect clearly in his conversation with Ophelia:

Ophelia Good my lord,
How does your honour for this many a day?

Hamlet I humbly thank you, well.

Ophelia My lord, I have remembrances of yours
That I have longed long to redeliver.
I pray you now receive them.

Ophelia, painfully aware that Polonius and Claudius are listening behind the arras, follows the instructions of her father to reject Hamlet's advances. To Hamlet—who has probably not abandoned all hope of winning over Ophelia—her words are like a painful lashing, and he reacts by pouring out all the bitterness within him.

Hamlet	No, not I. I never gave you aught.

This, of course, is essentially a lie. It may be just a bitter reaction to Ophelia wanting to return his gifts, thus affirming her resolve to reject him. But Hamlet may also be suggesting here that he is now so transformed that he is no longer his former self, the one who gave the gifts. Alternatively, he may be hinting that Ophelia is so changed that she is no longer the same person who received the gifts earlier.

Ophelia	My honoured lord, you know right well you did, And with them words of so sweet breath composed As made the things more rich. Their perfume lost, Take these again; for to the noble mind Rich gifts wax poor when givers prove unkind. There, my lord.
Hamlet	Ha, ha! Are you honest?
Ophelia	My lord?
Hamlet	Are you fair?

In the midst of all the deception and counter-deception, Hamlet, in his bitter state, suddenly cuts to the point—that Ophelia is neither being honest nor fair. Hamlet is too astute not to realize that the change in Ophelia's attitude is too sudden, and that she is not being entirely honest. In the dialogue, Shakespeare brings together the two recurring motifs of the lack of honesty and the tendency to beautify reality falsely.

Ophelia	What means your lordship?
Hamlet	That if you be honest and fair, your honesty should admit no discourse to your beauty.

When questioned directly about what he means, Hamlet reverts to his sardonic wit and delivers another of his enigmatic remarks, full of double meanings and innuendoes. It is a play on both "honest" and "fair." Honesty, in Shakespeare's time, is often used as a term to represent chastity, and fair, of course, also means beauty. Thus Hamlet is saying that if she is chaste, she should not allow anyone access to her beauty.

There is a deeper meaning which amplifies the play's thematic resonance. For we have, once again, an image of the "vile phrase" in the word "beautified." In one sense, Hamlet is referring to Ophelia's use of cosmetics to beautify and suggesting that this is not being honest. But it is also a general statement that artificially beautifying reality is not being honest.

Ophelia Could beauty, my lord, have better commerce than with honesty?

Ophelia says basically that beauty and honesty should go together. Hamlet now turns this on its head with a play on the word "commerce," and states that beauty has the better deal:

Hamlet Ay, truly; for the power of beauty will sooner transform honesty from what it is to a bawd than the force of honesty can translate beauty into his likeness. This was sometime[20] a paradox,[21] but now the time gives it proof.

Shakespeare homes in again on the recurring motif of falsely beautifying things to hide the truth. And certainly, here, beauty wins over honesty. Through our artificial beautification of reality, we lose our honesty to see the truth.

Hamlet I did love you once.

Ophelia Indeed, my lord, you made me believe so.

Hamlet You should not have believed me; for virtue cannot so inoculate our old stock but we shall relish of it. I loved you not.

Ophelia I was the more deceived.

---

20 **sometime** formerly

21 **paradox** statement contrary to accepted opinion

Hamlet is using the word "inoculate" in its etymological sense, being derived from the word "oculus," meaning bud. Employing a horticultural metaphor, he is therefore saying that merely engrafting a new stem of virtue onto an old immoral trunk will not eradicate all stains of our previous nature. Indeed, transforming our nature is a long, difficult process, and generally requires a purification by fire or a passage of trials and tribulations through prolonged perseverance. Although difficult, it is nonetheless our task in life to go through with it. Hamlet is definitely not suggesting here that we cannot transform ourselves, for later, in Scene 4, he practically gives instructions to his mother on how to do it and ends by saying: "For use almost can change the stamp of nature, and either the devil or throw him out with wondrous potency."

Hamlet now launches into a diatribe on the nature of man. In a way, this is a continuation to his soliloquy, a further comment on the perception of reality he has obtained by confronting the profound. Here, he describes the nature of man, stripped of all the "cosmetics" we lay on to beautify him. This is the aspect of reality—the sinful nature of our behavior—that Jesus focused on in his teachings, while the other aspect of reality—the suffering nature of our mundane life—was what the Buddha focused on. Generally, we ignore or artificially beautify both aspects of the truth because we simply refuse to face them. As a result, we wander through life lost in a fog of self-created delusions.

Hamlet, however, has had the courage to face the true nature of our existence, and this should have helped him onto the spiritual path. Unfortunately, this proper progression has been thwarted because he has adopted a path of vengeance and a path of condemning others. His reaction to the realization of the truth is thus all wrong.

When we do finally succeed in facing reality, we should respond in this way: The realization that our mundane lives are of the nature of suffering should make us renounce our worldly goals and turn instead to the higher aspirations of the spiritual path. The realization that our behavior is basically immoral should spur us on to transforming ourselves to a higher purity.

Both these responses correspond to Jesus' call for *metanoia*, a Greek word rather inadequately translated in the Bible as "repentance." *Meta* means transformation, and *noia* means being; so *metanoia* actually means the transformation of our being, or what in Buddhism is known as the "turning-about." This means more than just repentance of transgressions. It means a transformation of the mind to one that no longer seeks the mundane but is focused entirely on higher spiritual aspirations. This requires a mind of love and deep compassion—an impossible task for one bent on revenge and on the condemnation of others.

Because Hamlet's focus is on vengeance, we now witness the use of his realization of the nature of man in a most inappropriate way—as a form of attack to hurt Ophelia:

Hamlet	Get thee to a nunnery. Why wouldst thou be a breeder of sinners? I am myself indifferent honest, but yet I could accuse me of such things that it were better my mother had not borne me. I am very proud, revengeful, ambitious, with more offences at my beck than I have thoughts to put them in, imagination to give them shape, or time to act them in. What should such fellows as I do crawling between earth and heaven? We are arrant knaves all; believe none of us. Go thy ways to a nunnery.

A person goes to a nunnery to seek spiritual transformation, not to escape, as Hamlet suggests. Although what he says about the nature of man is basically true, he is inappropriately using it to taunt Ophelia. The proper response to this realization should be to inwardly seek to transform our own nature to a higher state, and to be compassionate to others who are basically in the same predicament. This, however, is simply not possible for Hamlet because he is focused on vengeance and on condemning others.

Note that Hamlet includes being revengeful as one of the failings of his nature, suggesting he inwardly knows that revenge is wrong.

Hamlet	Where is your father?
Ophelia	At home, my lord.
Hamlet	Let the doors be shut upon him, that he may play the fool nowhere but in's own house. Farewell.
Ophelia	Oh, help him, you sweet heavens!

Hamlet's sudden question concerning Ophelia's father has generated much speculation among critics that he now spies Polonius hiding behind the arras. There are, however, few grounds for this, given Hamlet's propensity for unexpected statements, especially when putting on his "antic disposition." An equivalent example would be "For if the sun breed maggots in a dead dog, being a good kissing carrion—Have you a daughter?"

Also, Elizabethan dramatic convention, and certainly Shakespeare, would have made Hamlet's awareness of being spied upon explicit, if this indeed were his intention. Shakespeare is very dramatic in presenting his meaning because he wants us to experience it directly. Therefore, if he does not make something explicit when it could have been so easily done, we can safely conclude he did not intend that meaning. Furthermore, if Hamlet did indeed spot Polonius behind the curtains here, it would be hard to justify later in Scene 4 why he so rashly concludes that it is the King, not Polonius, behind the arras.

The idea of Hamlet spotting Polonius here in Scene 1, was introduced to justify Hamlet's savagery in his treatment of Ophelia. This, however, detracts from the very point that Shakespeare is trying to make, which is that Hamlet *is* becoming more and more savage. The process is unmistakably consistent. In Scene 2, Hamlet continues his insulting behavior toward Ophelia, begins to openly taunt Rosencrantz and Guildenstern, and even thinks of killing his mother. In Scene 3, he refrains, out of sheer malice, from killing Claudius while he is praying because he would rather send him to hell. And in Scene 4, his savagery reaches such a brutal level that he persists in taunting Polonius even after he is dead. Then, in the following Act, he gets even worse, hiding Polonius's body and making macabre jokes about it.

Why then do we need to introduce something trivial to justify Hamlet's savagery here in Scene 1, when we have no hope of doing the same in all these subsequent scenes? We must accept the idea that Shakespeare *is* deliberately portraying Hamlet as becoming savage, and for a good reason. Hamlet is slowly but surely transforming into the image of the avenger, the one "roasted in wrath and fire, and thus o'ersized with coagulate gore, with eyes like carbuncles." He is transforming into the very image of the "hellish Pyrrhus."

Shakespeare's reason for Hamlet's question about Polonius and his following statement is to demonstrate Hamlet's response to the realization of the true nature of man. Immediately after admitting to his own failings, he nonetheless proceeds to condemn another. This illogical behavior is the result of a mind bent on vengeance, a mind bent on the aspect of justice that argues for another's punishment, completely contradicting the spiritual path of compassion. Now Hamlet proceeds to use his understanding of the nature of man to attack Ophelia herself:

Hamlet If thou dost marry, I'll give thee this plague for thy dowry: be thou chaste as ice, as pure as snow, thou shalt not escape calumny. Get thee to a nunnery, farewell.

This taunt by Hamlet is evidently fuelled by the bitter thought of Ophelia marrying someone other than himself. Ironically, the "plague" he bestows on Ophelia is a counter-statement to the earlier advice, by Polonius and Laertes, on how she may avoid calumny—the very advice that led her to reject Hamlet.

Hamlet's statement, however, does reflect a perverse nature of man: When good fortune embraces another, we are often envious and unhappy; when misfortune strikes another, we are often secretly pleased. It is hardly surprising, then, that one's reputation is always in danger of being tainted by others at the slightest opportunity. Ideally, each of us should focus on becoming a better person without any concern for reputation, which is a worldly concern.

Hamlet's pronouncement here does come close to the truth; his error, however, is in using it as a contemptuous gibe.

Hamlet Or if thou wilt needs marry, marry a fool; for wise men know well enough what monsters you make of them. To a nunnery, go and quickly too. Farewell.

Ophelia Heavenly powers, restore him!

Here is another of Hamlet's statements with a double meaning. By monsters, he may mean cuckolds, which are popularly supposed to sprout horns. But the statement may also mean the deterioration of the man into something worse because of the influence of the wife.

Hamlet I have heard of your paintings well enough. God hath given you one face and you make yourselves another. You jig and amble, and you lisp, you nickname God's creatures, and make your wantonness your ignorance. Go to, I'll no more on't, it hath made me mad.

Here, we return to the image of defects being concealed and "beautified." The use of cosmetics to hide the blemishes of the face is Shakespeare's metaphor for our inability to confront reality. We, too, conceal the truth—the true nature of both our existence and our character—by deluding ourselves and beautifying it with false images of our lives and of our nature. And in our incredible ability to hide from the inevitability of death, we display what *The Mahabhrata* calls the greatest wonder. Thus, in this cloud of delusion, we "jig and amble" through life, make affected speeches, use euphemisms ("nickname God's creatures"), and generally make "our wantonness our ignorance." This last phrase means that our wantonness is the result of our deliberately choosing to be ignorant of the truth.

When Hamlet says "it hath made me mad," he brings up yet another recurring motif in the play: Who is actually mad? Is it Hamlet, who has seen through the layer of false beautification, or is it we who continue to live in a state of delusion?

Hamlet I say we will have no more marriages. Those that are married already, all but one, shall live; the rest shall keep as they are. To a nunnery, go. [*Exit*]

In Hamlet's closing remarks, Shakespeare tells us again that Hamlet, after confronting the truth, has taken the wrong turn. He has become cynical, bitter, and savage. The reason can be found in the statement itself: it alludes to his condemnation of the remarriage of his mother, his vow of revenge, and constitutes a veiled threat to his uncle. Hamlet is transforming into the terrifying image of the avenger, the "hellish Pyrrhus." What he was before, we do not actually see in the play because even in Act I, he has already been changed by the bitter condemnation of his mother's remarriage. It is left to Ophelia to tell us:

Ophelia Oh, what a noble mind is here o'erthrown!
The courtier's, soldier's, scholar's, eye, tongue, sword,
Th'expectancy and rose of the fair state,

The glass of fashion and the mould of form,
Th'observed of all observers, quite, quite down!
And I, of ladies most deject and wretched,
That sucked the honey of his music vows,
Now see that noble and most sovereign reason
Like sweet bells jangled out of tune and harsh,
That unmatched form and feature of blown youth
Blasted with ecstasy.[22] Oh woe is me
T'have seen what I have seen, see what I see.

The pain of Ophelia reflects the tragedy of Hamlet's transformation. This is the real tragedy of the play: the transformation of one with the sensitivity, courage, and intellect to reach great heights of spiritual attainment into one oppressed with bitterness, cynicism, and brutality.

The King, too, is suitably alarmed by this change in Hamlet:

King Love? His affections[23] do not that way tend,
Nor what he spake, though it lacked form a little,
Was not like madness. There's something in his soul
O'er which his melancholy sits on brood,
And I do doubt[24] the hatch and disclose
Will be some danger; which for to prevent
I have in quick determination
Thus set it down: he shall with speed to England
For the demand of our neglected tribute.
Haply the seas and countries different,
With variable objects, shall expel
This something-settled matter in his heart,
Whereon his brains still beating puts him thus
From fashion of himself. What think you on't?

Claudius thus resolves to send Hamlet to England, and though he pretends that it is out of concern for Hamlet's health, it is more to keep him at bay after hearing his veiled threat. Polonius, however, is still fixated on his own theory of Hamlet's transformation.

---

22 **ecstasy** madness

23 **affections** emotions, inclinations

24 **doubt** fear

Polonius It shall do well. But yet do I believe
The origin and commencement of his grief
Sprung from neglected love. How now, Ophelia?
You need not tell us what Lord Hamlet said,
We heard it all. My lord, do as you please,
But if you hold it fit, after the play
Let his queen-mother all alone entreat him
To show his grief: let her be round[25] with him,
And I'll be placed, so please you, in the ear
Of all their conference. If she find him not,
To England send him; or confine him where
Your wisdom best shall think.

The game of deception and counter-deception continues, and the plans are set for the fateful closet scene. Before that, however, it will be Hamlet's turn to do the spying. The scene now closes with a remarkable statement by the King:

King It shall be so.
Madness in great ones must not unwatched go.

Here, in the King's closing remark, is a touch of incredible irony, for in the next scene, it is Claudius himself who will be closely watched. The statement also brings up again the thematic resonance on the question of madness. We know that Hamlet's madness is, at least to a large extent, put on. The King's action in murdering his own brother and taking his crown, however, is truly an act of delusion, an act of madness stemming from a blatant refusal to face the truth of his own mortality. In a masterstroke of Shakespearean irony, Hamlet and Horatio in the next scene clearly heed the King's own words that "madness in great ones must not unwatched go."

---

25 **round** blunt and direct

Scene 2

Scene 2 opens at the preparations for Hamlet's improvised play. Hamlet is instructing the actors:

Hamlet Suit the action to the word, the word to the action, with this special observance, that you o'erstep not the modesty of nature. For anything so o'erdone is from[26] the purpose of playing, whose end, both at the first and now, was and is to hold as 'twere the mirror up to nature; to show virtue her own feature, scorn her own image, and the very age and body of the time his form and pressure.[27] Now this overdone, or come tardy off, though it makes the unskilful laugh, cannot but make the judicious grieve, the censure of the which one must in your allowance o'erweigh a whole theatre of others.

While these may reflect Shakespeare's own instructions to his actors, they also inform us how to approach his plays. As their purpose is "to hold as 'twere the mirror up to nature," we should experience the action as though it were real. For the essence of Shakespeare's art lies in the creation of an intense experience within us, allowing us to learn from it as though we have lived it.

There is, however, another meaning to Hamlet's advice to the players. It serves as a metaphor of the world as the stage and we the actors. The performers' failing to mirror reality corresponds to our failing to live in accordance with the truth. This touches again the theme resonating throughout the play: our tendency to hide from the profound. If we run from the truth, we will live in a state of distraction, racing after meaningless goals, like a stage performance that does not match reality. We will behave like the clowns Hamlet now describes:

Hamlet And let those that play your clowns speak no more than is set down for them; for there be of them that will themselves laugh, to set on some quantity of barren spectators to laugh too, though in the

26 **from** contrary to

27 **pressure** impression (as of a seal), image

meantime some necessary question of the play be then to be considered. That's villainous, and shows a most pitiful ambition in the fool that uses it.

If we immerse ourselves in distractions rather than face reality, we may be so caught in worldly concerns that we miss the meaning of our lives. Then we are like the clowns indulging in irrelevant gags while disregarding the plot.

Since critics complain that Shakespeare himself indulges in scenes irrelevant to the main action, is it not incredible that Shakespeare has Hamlet disparage similar foolish behavior by wayward clowns? It certainly appears that Shakespeare is now chastising himself for such folly, and that he would consider it foolish to include extraneous scenes that merely entertain but are irrelevant—similar to how the thoughtless clowns spoil the show.

What we need to realize, however, is that Shakespeare is actually informing us that there are no extraneous scenes in his plays! Those scenes are important to the meaning of the play. It is a mistake to consider scenes he deliberately includes as being irrelevant because these scenes have a purpose. They are focused allegorical scenes that artistically amplify the meaning of the play.

Back at the scene, Horatio soon enters and Hamlet converses privately with him. We learn that Hamlet has taken him into his confidence:

Hamlet Since my dear soul was mistress of her choice,
And could of men distinguish her election,
Hath sealed thee for herself; for thou hast been
As one, in suff'ring all, that suffers nothing,
A man that Fortune's buffets and rewards
Hast ta'en with equal thanks; and blest are those
Whose blood[28] and judgement are so well co-mingled
That they are not a pipe for Fortune's finger
To sound what stop she please. Give me that man
That is not passion's slave, and I will wear him
In my heart's core, ay, in my heart of hearts,
As I do thee.

---

28 **blood** passion

Hamlet thus explains why he holds Horatio as his close friend. He sees in Horatio the steadfastness of one so familiar with suffering that it no longer affects him adversely. He is not one easily swayed by the swirls of fortune, or one whose judgment is hostage to passion. In praising these traits, however, Hamlet contradicts his earlier self-reproach for his own lack of passion in pursuing revenge. Our actions should be guided by spiritual principles and not by the caprice of passion. The approval of Horatio's steadfastness also introduces the principle that we cannot rely on the surges of momentary passion to carry us to our ideals. This theme recurs throughout the scene.

Hamlet continues:

Hamlet There is a play tonight before the King:
One scene of it comes near the circumstance
Which I have told thee of my father's death.
I prithee, when thou seest that act afoot,
Even with the very comment of thy soul
Observe my uncle. If his occulted[29] guilt
Do not itself unkennel[30] in one speech,
It is a damned ghost that we have seen,
And my imaginations are as foul
As Vulcan's stithy.[31] Give him heedful note;
For I mine eyes will rivet to his face,
And after we will both our judgements join
In censure of his seeming.[32]

Horatio Well, my lord.
If he steal aught the whilst this play is playing
And scape detecting, I will pay the theft.

Hamlet They are coming to the play. I must be idle.
Get you a place.

The tables are now turned, as the thematic resonance on deception and counter-deception continues. In the last scene, Hamlet was secretly

---

29 **occulted** hidden

30 **unkennel** bring into the open

31 **stithy** forge

32 **censure of his seeming** reaching a verdict on his appearance

observed under contrived circumstances; here he spies on Claudius in yet another contrived situation. The King and Queen now arrive with Polonius, Ophelia, Rosencrantz, and Guildenstern.

King How fares our cousin Hamlet?

Hamlet Excellent, i'faith, of the chameleon's dish. I eat the air, promise-crammed. You cannot feed capons so.

Chameleons were supposed to live on air. As usual, Hamlet's enigmatic remark is replete with double meanings. It suggests he is being fed empty promises and is dissatisfied with the question of succession to the throne. Thus he may be misleading Claudius on the reason for his discontent.

More likely however, this statement relates to the recurring theme in this scene: that one cannot rely on temporary passions to attain one's goals, spiritual or otherwise. Thus Hamlet may be referring to his own procrastination, his feeding on unfulfilled promises made only at times of passion. These promises are like the air, without substance. He also likens himself to a chameleon that transforms at times of emotional zeal and then cools off. Capons are castrated cocks fattened for the table, and Hamlet's reference to them may be another self-derogatory remark.

There is, however, a deeper meaning in relation to the spiritual path. We are likened to capons because we are all destined to die, destined to suffer the dissolution of our worldly possessions and attainments. Our redemption lies in the spiritual path, but we cannot succeed by moving along it only at times of passion, times which cannot be sustained. Thus we have, instead, to answer Jesus' call for *metanoia*, a call to transform our entire being into one focused purely on spiritual aspirations. There is no other way. By relying only on temporary passions to motivate us, we cannot succeed; like capons, we cannot live off air crammed with empty promises.

King I have nothing with this answer, Hamlet. These words are not mine.

Hamlet No, nor mine now.

By saying that he has "nothing with this answer," the King evidently means that Hamlet's words are not relevant to him, in the sense that they do not relate to his question. It is, however, also true in another way, since Claudius is not even motivated towards any goals, spiritual or otherwise.

He is too busy drowning himself in revelry and distractions, trying to hide from the truth.

Hamlet's reply again has a double meaning. It may simply mean that the words no longer belong to him since they have left his lips. Alternatively, it may mean that he is determined not to continue living on empty promises; instead, he is ready for action. Hamlet now turns to Polonius:

Hamlet	My lord, you played once i'th'university, you say?
Polonius	That did I, my lord, and was accounted a good actor.
Hamlet	What did you enact?
Polonius	I did enact Julius Caesar. I was killed i'th'Capitol. Brutus killed me.
Hamlet	It was a brute part of him to kill so capital a calf there.

Reference is made again to Shakespeare's other play, *Julius Caesar*, and we are reminded once more of its central theme: the error of not aligning oneself with one's true spiritual nature and with the divine. Recall that Brutus takes part in the conspiracy to murder Caesar purely from intellectual considerations, without seeking guidance from the deeper spiritual tides within himself, and hence without seeking to flow with the Tao. In this way, even with what appears to be a good motive, Brutus makes a dire mistake. So Hamlet is appropriate, here, in saying that it was the "brute part of him" that acted thus. Ironically, Hamlet himself makes the same error. He fails to heed the deeper spiritual voice within, crying out that revenge is wrong. He hesitates because of it but fails to recognize explicitly why he delays.

The play within the play is about to begin:

Hamlet	Be the players ready?
Rosencrantz	Ay, my lord, they stay upon your patience.
Queen	Come hither, my dear Hamlet, sit by me.
Hamlet	No, good mother, here's metal more attractive. [*Turns to Ophelia*]
Polonius	[*Aside to the King*] Oh ho! Do you mark that?

Hamlet evidently chooses not to sit next to the Queen because he requires a good view of the King during the play. However, by sitting with Ophelia instead, he inadvertently fuels Polonius's assumption that his malady is the result of spurned love. It also allows Shakespeare to show that Hamlet's mistreatment of Ophelia in the last scene was no temporary misbehavior, for Hamlet now sustains this lack of consideration by mouthing a string of insensitive lewd remarks:

Hamlet	[*Lying down at Ophelia's feet*] Lady, shall I lie in your lap?
Ophelia	No, my lord.
Hamlet	I mean, my head upon your lap.
Ophelia	Ay, my lord.
Hamlet	Do you think I meant country matters?
Ophelia	I think nothing, my lord.
Hamlet	That's a fair thought to lie between maids' legs.
Ophelia	What is, my lord?
Hamlet	Nothing.

To "lie in your lap" has sexual innuendoes that Ophelia clearly recognizes. Hamlet then pretends that this was not his meaning, and asks Ophelia whether she was thinking of "country matters." This, in itself, has a further sexual connotation, with a pun on the first syllable. Hamlet continues with further ribald remarks about lying between maids' legs. All this may be appropriate for a bawdy tavern scene, but is hardly proper here for Ophelia, the tame filial daughter who plays by the rules. This lewd, mocking conversation displays Hamlet's attitude towards her now: cynical and taunting, with a scarcely masked desire to hurt.

Ophelia	You are merry, my lord.
Hamlet	Who, I?
Ophelia	Ay, my lord.

Hamlet Oh God, your only jig-maker![33] What should a man do but be merry? For look you how cheerfully my mother looks and my father died within's two hours.

After calling himself a jig-maker, with the self-derogatory suggestion that he is wasting time on trivialities instead of taking firm action, Hamlet turns his taunts toward his mother.

Ophelia Nay, 'tis twice two months, my lord.

Hamlet So long? Nay then, let the devil wear black, for I'll have a suit of sables.

Sables are dark furs, and the word is the heraldic term for black. Hamlet continues his cynical taunting, yet his remark has a deeper meaning. It is the devil, the king of mischief, who merely wears black—signifying a superficial show of mourning—while Hamlet takes on the deeper and richer sables—signifying the profound inner acknowledgement of his father's death and the reality of death itself. It is an apt statement, for it is the denial of our mortality that allows the folly of evil to exist—the folly of wasting our lives grasping after worldly attractions and achievements that inexorably end in dust.

Hamlet Oh heavens, die two months ago and not forgotten yet! Then there's hope a great man's memory may outlive his life half a year. But by'r lady he must build churches then, or else he suffer not thinking on, with the hobbyhorse, whose epitaph is, 'For O, for O, the hobby-horse is forgot.'

Hamlet's taunts bite, for they do echo truth. Our worldly achievements amount to little after our departure, and like the hobby-horse are soon forgotten. The hobby-horse is a character in the morris-dance at summer festivities, consisting of a figure of a horse fastened around the waist of a man whose legs are concealed by a ring of cloth hanging from the horse. False legs are attached to the sides of the horse, so that the man appears to be riding on it when he is actually walking around. This image of a half-man, half-beast signifies man's more bestial nature, which is appropriately

---

33 **jig-maker** composer or performer of comical song-and-dance routines

not worth remembering. We will meet this motif of a half-man, half-beast again in Act IV.

The trumpets now sound and the play-within-the-play begins with a dumb show:

Enter a King and a Queen, very lovingly, the Queen embracing him and he her. She kneels, and makes show of protestation unto him. He takes her up, and declines his head upon her neck. He lies him down upon a bank of flowers. She, seeing him asleep, leaves him. Anon comes in another Man, takes off his crown, kisses it, pours poison in the sleeper's ears, and leaves him. The Queen returns, finds the King dead, makes passionate action. The Poisoner with some Three or Four comes in again. They seem to condole with her. The dead body is carried away. The Poisoner woos the Queen with gifts. She seems harsh awhile, but in the end accepts his love.

Ophelia What means this, my lord?

Hamlet Marry, this is miching[34] malicho.[35] It means mischief.

Ophelia Belike this show imports the argument of the play.

Commentators have noted that this dumb show is unusual because it exactly mimes what follows in the play. This leaves a long-standing problem: Why does the King not react to the dumb show? It is clearly not an oversight by Shakespeare, since he has Ophelia directly ask what the show means and whether it imports the argument of the play. Together with Hamlet's answer that it represents mischief, the audience is clearly informed that the dumb show does, in fact, import the argument of the play. Thus Shakespeare intentionally highlights the dumb show and the King's non-reaction. Why?

Since Shakespeare is drawing our attention to the dumb show, we can dismiss suggestions that the King either fails to see the show or is unable to recognize its meaning. Shakespeare is instead making a point with the King's non-reaction: Claudius does not react to the dumb show because he denies what it represents.

---

34 **miching** lurking or being furtive

35 **malicho** probably refers either to the Italian word malocchio which means the evil eye, or the Spanish word malhecho which means wrongdoing.

The King simply refuses to confront the truth, just as most of us refuse to accept the inevitability of death. It is well known in psychology that the first reaction on being told of one's terminal illness is to deny it. The King reacts in a similar way to the dumb show. Having little forewarning that Hamlet knows of his father's murder, the King denies that the dumb show has anything to do with it. It is only later, when Hamlet virtually forces it upon him, that he is genuinely frightened. This is Shakespeare in his artistic element. Just as he provided us with a dramatic depiction of the nature of revenge in the speech on Pyrrhus, he now presents us with a dramatic portrayal of another main theme resonating throughout the play: our tendency to deny reality and to hide from the truth.

Back at the scene, the Prologue now enters. Hamlet's dialogue with Ophelia continues to focus on the meaning of the dumb show, until he diverts it with another lewd remark, clearly aimed at discomforting Ophelia:

Hamlet We shall know by this fellow. The players cannot keep counsel: they'll tell all.

Ophelia Will he tell us what this show meant?

Hamlet Ay, or any show that you will show him. Be not you ashamed to show, he'll not shame to tell you what it means.

Ophelia You are naught,[36] you are naught. I'll mark the play.

Prologue *For us and for our tragedy,*
Here stooping to your clemency,
We beg your hearing patiently. [*Exit*]

Hamlet Is this a prologue, or the posy[37] of a ring?

Ophelia 'Tis brief, my lord.

Hamlet As woman's love.

Another sardonic remark by Hamlet that reveals a mind bent on vengeance. He is full of bitterness and condemnation and can hardly

---

36 **naught** wicked

37 **posy** inscribed motto

refrain from insulting those around him. This statement strikes out at both the Queen and Ophelia herself.

The Player King now enters with the Player Queen and tells of their love and marriage for thirty years. The Player Queen strongly professes her love and how her concern over his recent poor health reflects it. The Player King continues:

Player King *Faith, I must leave thee, love, and shortly too:*
My operant[38] *powers their functions leave to do;*
And thou shalt live in this fair world behind,
Honoured, beloved; and haply one as kind
For husband shalt thou—

Player Queen *O confound the rest.*
Such love must needs be treason in my breast.
In second husband let me be accurst;
None wed the second but who killed the first.

Hamlet [*Aside*] That's wormwood.[39]

Player Queen *The instances*[40] *that second marriage move*
Are base respects of thrift,[41] *but none of love.*
A second time I kill my husband dead,
When second husband kisses me in bed.

Hamlet has clearly organized the play not only to catch the conscience of the King, as he puts it, but also to openly condemn the hasty remarriage of his mother. Much of the play is targeted at her.

Player King *I do believe you think what now you speak;*
But what we do determine, oft we break.
Purpose is but the slave to memory,
Of violent birth but poor validity,
Which now, the fruit unripe, sticks on the tree,
But fall unshaken when they mellow be.
Most necessary 'tis that we forget

---

38 **operant** active

39 **wormwood** *Artemisia absinthium*, a bitter herb

40 **instances** motives

41 **respects of thrift** considerations of advantage

To pay ourselves what to ourselves is debt.
What to ourselves in passion we propose,
The passion ending, doth the purpose lose.
The violence of either grief or joy
Their own enactures[42] *with themselves destroy.*
Where joy most revels grief doth most lament;
Grief joys, joy grieves, on slender accident.

Shakespeare returns to the theme that one cannot feed capons on air filled with empty promises. If we only strive on the spiritual path at times of passion, we have little hope of succeeding. What is required is a transformation of our being to one that naturally and consistently struggles for the spiritual ideal.

Ironically, this principle also applies to Hamlet on the path of vengeance. He cannot succeed on firm resolve only at times of passion; he has to focus on it all the time. Thus, he must transform himself into the very image of the hellish Pyrrhus, the image of the terrible avenger, and we are beginning to see his dreadful transformation on this dark road to desolation.

The Player King continues:

Player King *This world is not for aye, nor 'tis not strange*
That even our loves should with our fortunes change,
For 'tis a question left us yet to prove,
Whether love lead fortune or else fortune love.
The great man down, you mark his favourite flies;
The poor advanced makes friends of enemies;
And hitherto doth love on fortune tend:
For who not needs shall never lack a friend,
And who in want a hollow friend doth try
Directly seasons him[43] *his enemy.*

We may view this question of "whether love lead fortune or else fortune love" at two levels. One level is the Player King's example: Does our choice of friendship depend on the wealth of the person and hence on our ability to benefit materially from it?

---

42 **enactures** acts

43 **seasons him** converts him into

At a deeper level, the question of "whether love lead fortune or else fortune love" is actually our trial on Earth: Will our desire for the worldly divert us from our true mission in life? To ensure we do not fall into this trap, we must face the profound, and accept reality, without our contrivances to "beautify" the rottenness within. We need to recognize the unsatisfactory nature of worldly attractions, for they are temporary at best. We need to accept that even our life is temporary. By acknowledging the truth, we will realize the futility of striving for riches and reputation in this mundane world. Thus, we must perceive reality with unhampered clarity if we are to avoid squandering our life on futile pursuits.

Hamlet has managed to get this far in his spiritual development, but he has been tragically waylaid by the pernicious ideas of vengeance and of condemning others. The play now returns to the theme of condemning the Queen's remarriage.

Player King *But orderly to end where I begun,*
Our wills and fates do so contrary run
That our devices still are overthrown:
Our thoughts are ours, their ends none of our own.
So think thou wilt no second husband wed,
But die thy thoughts when thy first lord is dead.

Player Queen *Nor earth to me give food, nor heaven light,*
Sport and repose lock from me day and night,
To desperation turn my trust and hope,
An anchor's[44] *cheer in prison be my scope,*
Each opposite that blanks[45] *the face of joy,*
Meet what I would have well and it destroy,
Both here and hence pursue me lasting strife,
If, once a widow, ever I be a wife.

Hamlet If she should break it now.

Player King *'Tis deeply sworn. Sweet, leave me here awhile.*
My spirits grow dull, and fain I would beguile
The tedious day with sleep.

---

44 **anchor** anchorite, hermit

45 **blanks** blanches, makes pale

Player Queen	*Sleep rock thy brain,* *And never come mischance between us twain.* [*Exit. He sleeps*]
Hamlet	Madam, how like you this play?
Queen	The lady doth protest too much, methinks.
Hamlet	Oh, but she'll keep her word.

Hamlet cannot resist further snide remarks at his mother. Steeped in bitter condemnation of others, he is wantonly hurling sarcasm at all around him: the King, the Queen, Polonius, and even Ophelia. Here, then, is a glimpse of the mind of an avenger.

The King now questions Hamlet about the play. He has witnessed the dumb show, and although initially denying its relevance to his own foul deed, he is nonetheless uneasy about the play. Hamlet forces the point on him.

King	Have you heard the argument?[46] Is there no offence in't?
Hamlet	No, no, they do but jest—poison in jest. No offence i'th'world.
King	What do you call the play?
Hamlet	The Mousetrap—marry, how tropically? This play is the image of a murder done in Vienna; Gonzago is the Duke's name, his wife Baptista; you shall see anon. 'Tis a knavish piece of work, but what o'that? Your Majesty, and we that have free souls, it touches us not. Let the galled jade wince, our withers are unwrung.

A "galled jade" is a horse that has been rubbed sore from a poorly fitting saddle, and "withers" is the highest part of the horse's back that is prone to this abuse. Hamlet's comment now compels the King to seriously consider that the play does indeed reflect his own misdeed. No longer can he simply deny it—the trap is ready to fall.

Now the actor playing Lucianus, the murderer, enters.

Hamlet	This is one Lucianus, nephew to the King.

46 **argument** plot

Here is a subtle but brilliant touch by Shakespeare. By making Lucianus the nephew to the victim—instead of brother—a parallel is drawn with the relationship now between Hamlet and his uncle, the King. It suggests that Hamlet, in seeking revenge, is taking on the characteristics of the original killer. The avenger, in reciprocating the action of the original murder, in many ways takes on the role of the original murderer.

Now Ophelia interjects and immediately becomes the target for further bawdy abuse by Hamlet:

Ophelia	You are as good as a chorus, my lord.
Hamlet	I could interpret between you and your love if I could see the puppets dallying.
Ophelia	You are keen, my lord, you are keen.
Hamlet	It would cost you a groaning to take off my edge.
Ophelia	Still better, and worse.
Hamlet	So you mistake your husbands.

A pun on the words "must take," makes a mockery of the traditional lines in the marriage vows. Now the "mousetrap" is released.

Hamlet Begin murderer. Leave thy damnable faces and begin. Come, the croaking raven doth bellow for revenge.

Lucianus
Thoughts black, hands apt, drugs fit, and time agreeing.
Confederate season,[47] *else no creature seeing.*
Thou mixture rank, of midnight weeds collected,
With Hecate's[48] *ban*[49] *thrice blasted, thrice infected,*
Thy natural magic and dire property
On wholesome life usurps immediately.
[*Pours the poison in the sleeper's ears*]

Hamlet He poisons him i'th'garden for his estate. His name's Gonzago. The story is extant, and written in very choice Italian. You shall see anon how the murderer gets the love of Gonzago's wife.

---

47 **confederate season** the occasion assisting me

48 **Hecate** goddess of witchcraft

49 **ban** curse

Ophelia The King rises.

Hamlet What, frighted with false fire?

Queen How fares my lord?

Polonius Give o'er the play.

King Give me some light. Away.

Polonius Lights, lights, lights.

The trap is sprung. The King has revealed his guilt, and Hamlet's reaction is significant. He is not dismayed that his uncle is as guilty as the ghost informs. Instead, he exults. His mind is already so bitter and bent on revenge that he feels triumphant at the success of his trap.

Hamlet
Why, let the strucken deer go weep,
The hart ungalled play;
For some must watch while some must sleep,
Thus runs the world away.
Would not this, sir, and a forest of feathers, if the rest of my fortunes turn Turk[50] with me, with two Provincial roses on my razed shoes,[51] get me a fellowship in a cry[52] of players?

Horatio Half a share.

Hamlet A whole one, I.
For thou dost know, Oh Damon dear,
This realm dismantled was
Of Jove himself, and now reigns here
A very, very—pajock.

Horatio You might have rhymed.

Horatio obviously expected the rhyming word to be "ass." Pajock is an unknown word; it may refer to "patchock," a word used by Spencer in *A View of the Present State of Ireland*, suggesting a despicable person.

---

50 **turn Turk** renounce, desert

51 **razed shoes** shoes ornamented by slits

52 **cry** company

Hamlet Oh good Horatio, I'll take the ghost's word for a thousand pound. Didst perceive?

Horatio Very well, my lord.

Hamlet Upon the talk of the poisoning?

Horatio I did very well note him.

Hamlet Ah ha! Come, some music; come, the recorders.
For if the King like not the comedy,
Why then, belike he likes it not, perdy.[53]
Come, some music.

Now Rosencrantz and Guildenstern enter and immediately become the target of Hamlet's cynical jests. While there is still an air of triumphant exultation, Hamlet's taunts have become malicious and direct. He means to hurt.

Guildenstern Good my lord, vouchsafe me a word with you.

Hamlet Sir, a whole history.

Guildenstern The King, sir—

Hamlet Ay, sir, what of him?

Guildenstern Is in his retirement marvellous distempered.

Hamlet With drink, sir?

Hamlet sarcastically reminds us of the King's use of wanton revelry to escape from the profound. The dialogue now continues with cynically inappropriate replies from Hamlet, who hardly cares that Rosencrantz and Guildenstern recognize them as taunts.

Guildenstern No, my lord, with choler.[54]

Hamlet Your wisdom should show itself more richer to signify this to the doctor, for, for me to put him to his purgation would perhaps plunge him into more choler.

---

53 **perdy** French pardieu "by God"

54 **choler** anger. Hamlet, however, chooses to understand it as "bile".

Guildenstern Good my lord, put your discourse into some frame, and start not so wildly from my affair.

Hamlet I am tame, sir. Pronounce.

Guildenstern The Queen your mother, in most great affliction of spirit, hath sent me to you.

Hamlet You are welcome.

Guildenstern Nay, good my lord, this courtesy is not of the right breed. If it shall please you to make me a wholesome answer, I will do your mother's commandment; if not, your pardon and my return shall be the end of my business.

Hamlet Sir, I cannot.

Rosencrantz What, my lord?

Hamlet Make you a wholesome answer. My wit's diseased. But sir, such answer as I can make, you shall command—or rather, as you say, my mother. Therefore no more, but to the matter. My mother, you say—

Rosencrantz Then thus she says: your behaviour hath struck her into amazement and admiration.[55]

Hamlet Oh wonderful son, that can so astonish a mother!

Hamlet's replies, while comical, are laced with bitter resentment at his former friends. He is openly treating them with contempt.

Hamlet But is there no sequel at the heels of this mother's admiration? Impart.

Rosencrantz She desires to speak with you in her closet ere you go to bed.

Hamlet We shall obey, were she ten times our mother. Have you any further trade with us?

---

55 **admiration** wonder

Rosencrantz now bluntly reveals that they are aware Hamlet is toying with them. Nonetheless, Hamlet persists with his cynical jests.

Rosencrantz My lord, you once did love me.

Hamlet And do still, by these pickers and stealers.[56]

Rosencrantz Good my lord, what is your cause of distemper? You do surely bar the door upon your own liberty if you deny your griefs to your friend.

Hamlet Sir, I lack advancement.

Rosencrantz How can that be, when you have the voice of the King himself for your succession in Denmark?

Hamlet Ay, sir, but while the grass grows—the proverb is something musty.

The proverb is "While the grass grows, the horse starves." Hamlet tries to mislead Rosencrantz and Guildenstern as to the cause of his strange behavior.

Players now enter with recorders, and Hamlet seizes the opportunity to enact a brilliant metaphor of how he is being treated. He is openly hostile to his former friends.

Hamlet Oh, the recorders. Let me see one. To withdraw with you, why do you go about to recover the wind[57] of me, as if you would drive me into a toil?[58]

Guildenstern Oh my lord, if my duty be too bold, my love is too unmannerly.

Guildenstern suggests that his boldness in questioning him is due to his love, which is the cause of this breach in good manners. Hamlet bluntly brushes that aside.

Hamlet I do not well understand that. Will you play upon this pipe?

---

56 **pickers and stealers** hands

57 **recover the wind** get on the windward side, as a hunter would, to drive his prey towards the trap.

58 **toil** snare

Guildenstern My lord, I cannot.

Hamlet I pray you.

Guildenstern Believe me, I cannot.

Hamlet I do beseech you.

Guildenstern I know no touch of it, my lord.

Hamlet It is as easy as lying. Govern these ventages[59] with your fingers and thumb, give it breath with your mouth, and it will discourse most eloquent music. Look you, these are the stops.

Guildenstern But these cannot I command to any utterance of harmony. I have not the skill.

Hamlet Why, look you now, how unworthy a thing you make of me. You would play upon me, you would seem to know my stops, you would pluck out the heart of my mystery, you would sound me from my lowest note to the top of my compass;[60] and there is much music, excellent voice, in this little organ, yet cannot you make it speak. Why, do you think I am easier to be played on than a pipe? Call me what instrument you will, though you can fret me, you cannot play upon me.

Hamlet thus dramatically rebukes Guildenstern for trying to play on him like an instrument. Now comes the irony. Polonius enters and Hamlet proceeds to do exactly what he just accused his former friend of trying to do. He plays upon Polonius, just like a pipe. The difference is that Hamlet does succeed, and Polonius is made to look utterly foolish.

Hamlet God bless you, sir.

Polonius My lord, the Queen would speak with you, and presently.

Hamlet Do you see yonder cloud that's almost in shape of a camel?

---

59 **ventages** vents, holes

60 **compass** range of voice

Polonius By th'mass and 'tis like a camel indeed.

Hamlet Methinks it is like a weasel.

Polonius It is backed like a weasel.

Hamlet Or like a whale.

Polonius Very like a whale.

Hamlet Then I will come to my mother by and by. [*Aside*] They fool me to the top of my bent.[61] I will come by and by.

Polonius I will say so.

Hamlet 'By and by' is easily said. Leave me, friends.

Hamlet is now alone and can freely speak his mind. We see directly the state he is in.

Hamlet 'Tis now the very witching time of night,
When churchyards yawn and hell itself breathes out
Contagion to this world. Now could I drink hot blood,
And do such bitter business as the day
Would quake to look on.

Hamlet has now fully taken on the role of the avenger, becoming the image of the hellish Pyrrhus. The effect is so great that even the thought of killing his mother enters his mind, and he must consciously suppress it.

Hamlet Soft, now to my mother.
Oh heart, lose not thy nature. Let not ever
The soul of Nero[62] enter this firm bosom;
Let me be cruel, not unnatural.
I will speak daggers to her, but use none.
My tongue and soul in this be hypocrites:
How in my words somever she be shent,[63]
To give them seals[64] never my soul consent.

---

61 **fool me to the top of my bent** force me to play the fool to the limit of my ability

62 **Nero** Roman emperor who had his mother murdered

63 **shent** abused, rebuked

64 **give them seals** confirm them with deeds

Scene 3

Scene 3 opens with the King, visibly shaken, instructing Guildenstern and Rosencrantz to escort Hamlet to England:

King I like it not; nor stands it safe with us
To let his madness range. Therefore prepare you.
I your commission will forthwith dispatch,
And he to England shall along with you.
The terms[65] of our estate[66] may not endure
Hazard so near us as doth hourly grow
Out of his brows.

Guildenstern We will ourselves provide.
Most holy and religious fear it is
To keep those many many bodies safe
That live and feed upon your Majesty.

Rosencrantz The single and peculiar life is bound
With all the strength and armour of the mind
To keep itself from noyance;[67] but much more
That spirit upon whose weal depends and rests
The lives of many. The cease of majesty
Dies not alone, but like a gulf doth draw
What's near it with it. It is a massy wheel
Fixed on the summit of the highest mount,
To whose huge spokes ten thousand lesser things
Are mortised and adjoined, which when it falls,
Each small annexment, petty consequence,
Attends the boist'rous ruin. Never alone
Did the King sigh, but with a general groan.

Ironically, it is Rosencrantz, the career man, who provides a brilliant imagery of the fate of the masses devoted purely to their worldly careers. Attached mindlessly to the spokes of an ever-turning wheel—here represented by the King, the source of worldly riches and power and also

[65] **terms** nature, condition

[66] **our estate** his position as king

[67] **noyance** injury

the villain himself—all will be dragged to the same ruin. The senseless whirl of materialistic ambition amounts to nothing in the end. And blind devotion to our worldly careers even becomes a means to hide from the profound. Then a vicious cycle is established, because it was our refusal to face reality that first caused the folly of wasting our lives grappling after material gains.

King Arm you, I pray you, to this speedy voyage,
For we will fetters put about this fear
Which now goes too free-footed.

Rosencrantz We will haste us.

After Rosencrantz and Guildenstern leave, Polonius enters and informs the King of his ill-fated plans to spy on the coming encounter between Hamlet and his mother.

Polonius My lord, he's going to his mother's closet.
Behind the arras I'll convey myself
To hear the process. I'll warrant she'll tax him home,[68]
And as you said—and wisely was it said—
'Tis meet that some more audience than a mother,
Since nature makes them partial, should o'erhear
The speech of vantage.[69] Fare you well, my liege.
I'll call upon you ere you go to bed.
And tell you what I know.

King Thanks, dear my lord.

Alone now, after Polonius leaves, the King openly reacts to his distress that Hamlet knows the dreaded truth. Unable to hide anymore from the horror of his deed, he finally attempts praying for redemption. Unfortunately, his motivation is purely one of self-interest, and is doomed to fail. Remorse arises only because of the danger now lurking around him.

King Oh, my offence is rank, it smells to heaven;
It hath the primal eldest curse[70] upon't—
A brother's murder! Pray can I not,

---

68 **tax him home** reprimand him severely

69 **of vantage** from an advantageous position

70 **primal elder's curse** curse of Cain, who murdered his brother Abel

Though inclination be as sharp as will,
My stronger guilt defeats my strong intent,
And, like a man to double business bound,
I stand in pause where I shall first begin,
And both neglect. What if this cursed hand
Were thicker than itself with brother's blood,
Is there not rain enough in the sweet heavens
To wash it white as snow? Whereto serves mercy
But to confront the visage of offence?
And what's in prayer but this twofold force,
To be forestalled ere we come to fall
Or pardoned being down? Then I'll look up.
My fault is past.

Claudius tries to convince himself that prayer offers him the hope of salvation. Something else, however, has to accompany it, as he soon realizes. Merely going through the motions of praying is insufficient.

King But oh, what form of prayer
Can serve my turn? 'Forgive me my foul murder'?
That cannot be, since I am still possessed
Of those effects for which I did the murder—
My crown, mine own ambition, and my queen.
May one be pardoned and retain th'offence?

Through this soliloquy, Shakespeare conveys what is needed on the spiritual path. It is not mere repentance as a sense of regret but *metanoia*[71]—the transformation of our being into the spiritual ideal—that is required.

The King craves forgiveness only because of concern for his own welfare. It is a purely selfish motivation and is insufficient.

King In the corrupted currents of this world
Offence's gilded hand may shove by justice,
And oft 'tis seen the wicked prize itself
Buys out the law. But 'tis not so above:
There is no shuffling,[72] there the action lies

---

71 For an explanation of *metanoia*, see pp. 99-100.

72 **shuffling** evasion

In his true nature, and we ourselves compelled
Even to the teeth and forehead of our faults
To give in evidence. What then? What rests?
Try what repentance can. What can it not?
Yet what can it, when one cannot repent?
Oh wretched state! Oh bosom black as death!
Oh limed[73] soul, that struggling to be free
Art more engaged![74] Help, angels! Make assay.[75]
Bow, stubborn knees; and heart with strings of steel,
Be soft as sinews of the new-born babe.
All may be well.

Hamlet enters and stumbles upon the King praying. He can now exact his revenge, but instead, he hesitates.

Hamlet Now might I do it pat, now he is a-praying.
And now I'll do't. [*Draws his sword*]
And so he goes to heaven;
And so am I revenged. That would be scanned:[76]
A villain kills my father, and for that
I, his sole son, do this same villain send
To heaven.
Why, this is hire and salary, not revenge.
He took my father grossly, full of bread,
With all his crimes broad blown,[77] as flush[78] as May;
And how his audit[79] stands who knows save heaven?
But in our circumstance and course of thought
'Tis heavy with him. And am I then revenged,
To take him in the purging of his soul,
When he is fit and seasoned for his passage?

---

73 **limed** caught (as with birdlime, a sticky substance used to catch birds)

74 **engaged** entangled

75 **assay** an attempt

76 **would be scanned** needs to be considered

77 **broad blown** in full bloom

78 **flush** vigorous

79 **audit** account

No.
Up, sword, and know thou a more horrid hent:[80]
When he is drunk asleep, or in his rage,
Or in th'incestuous pleasure of his bed,
At game a-swearing, or about some act
That has no relish[81] of salvation in't,
Then trip him, that his heels may kick at heaven,
And that his soul may be as damned and black
As hell whereto it goes. My mother stays.
This physic[82] but prolongs thy sickly days.

Hamlet's hesitation to kill the King is the critical action in this scene, and it serves two purposes. First, it reveals that Hamlet's motivation for revenge is not merely justice. It is vengeance in a purely malicious sense. He is out to make Claudius suffer. Hamlet has become the hellish Pyrrhus, thirsting for blood and the infliction of pain.

It is also a scene of incredible irony and aptly illustrates the nature of revenge. Here we have the villain struggling with guilt and craving redemption while the avenger plots the most hideous suffering for him. At this time, at least, the avenger is in a worse spiritual state than the villain himself.

The second purpose of this scene is to reinforce the true requirement for the spiritual path. Shakespeare has dramatically portrayed the absurdity of believing we will be heaven bound simply because we are praying when we die. If this were true, then the greatest act of love and sacrifice, on our part, must surely be to kill all people while they are praying. Indeed, what better deed can we do for our brothers and sisters? But this is patently absurd, just as it is absurd to believe that Hamlet truly had in his hands and through the act of murder the power to send Claudius to heaven.

What is required on the spiritual path is not merely the sense of regret for our misdeeds, but *metanoia*, the transformation of our being towards the spiritual ideal of universal love and compassion. This is the real meaning

80 **hent** occasion, opportunity

81 **relish** trace

82 **physic** remedy (i.e. Claudius' prayer)

of Jesus' call for "repentance." It is a call for a total transformation of our being and our motivation. It is a call to love our neighbor as ourselves.

Metanoia is required on the spiritual path because it is the transformation of our mind towards the spiritual ideal that enables us to directly experience the higher spiritual truths. As our mind transforms into one capable of receiving each higher spiritual truth, that truth will be revealed to us. Without this progressive direct realization of these truths, we cannot progress along the spiritual path.

The scene ends with Shakespeare informing us that, indeed, Hamlet could not have sent Claudius to heaven by killing him, even had he desired it.

King My words fly up, my thoughts remain below.
Words without thoughts never to heaven go.

Scene 4

Scene 4 takes us to the Queen's closet, where Polonius is preparing to conceal himself behind the arras.

Polonius He will come straight. Look you lay home to him,
Tell him his pranks have been too broad to bear with
And that your Grace hath screened and stood between
Much heat and him. I'll silence me even here.
Pray you be round with him.

It is with painful irony that Polonius's penchant for petty court intrigue, which distracts him from the profound, serves in the end to hurry his own encounter with the inevitable. His own ominous, prophetic words echo the irony: "I'll silence me even here."

Queen I'll warrant you, fear me not.
Withdraw, I hear him coming.

Hamlet, who has already worked himself into a fearsome mood, now enters to confront his mother.

Hamlet Now, mother, what's the matter?

Queen Hamlet, thou hast thy father much offended.

Hamlet Mother, you have my father much offended.

Queen Come, come, you answer with an idle tongue.

Hamlet Go, go, you question with a wicked tongue.

Queen Why, how now, Hamlet?

Hamlet What's the matter now?

Queen Have you forgot me?

Hamlet No, by the rood,[83] not so.
You are the Queen, your husband's brother's wife,
And, would it were not so, you are my mother.

Queen Nay, then I'll set those to you that can speak.

---

83 **rood** cross

Seeing Hamlet in a wildly defiant mood, the Queen prepares to leave. Hamlet now restrains her, causing her to cry out in distress.

Hamlet Come, come, and sit you down, you shall not budge.
You go not till I set you up a glass[84]
Where you may see the inmost part of you.

Queen What wilt thou do? Thou wilt not murder me?
Help, ho!

From behind the arras, an alarmed Polonius echoes the call for help and meets his fate.

Polonius What ho! Help!

Hamlet How now? A rat! Dead for a ducat, dead.

Hamlet, like the hellish Pyrrhus, is too ready to drink hot blood. In the fevered role of the avenger, imagining the King to be the hidden observer, Hamlet rashly plunges his rapier through the arras, killing Polonius.

Polonius [*Behind*] Oh, I am slain.

Queen Oh me, what hast thou done?

Hamlet Nay, I know not.
Is it the King?

Hamlet now lifts up the arras and discovers that he has killed Polonius, not the King. His reaction to this terrible discovery is truly telling for its lack of compassion for Polonius.

Queen Oh what a rash and bloody deed is this?

Hamlet A bloody deed. Almost as bad, good mother,
As kill a king and marry with his brother.

Hamlet's first words after the discovery of his horrible mistake still focus on revenge and on condemning his mother. There is little room for compassion.

Queen As kill a king?

Hamlet Ay, lady, it was my word.
Thou wretched, rash, intruding fool, farewell.

---

84 **glass** mirror

I took thee for thy better. Take thy fortune:
Thou find'st to be too busy is some danger.

To stress Hamlet's lack of remorse, Shakespeare even has Hamlet ridicule the slain Polonius. Compassion and vengeance are mutually exclusive, and innocent parties straying onto the bloody path of the avenger are often crushed with scant remorse.

Vengeance destroys the spiritual path, for the route to salvation requires universal love and compassion. If we exclude even one single being from this universality, the whole process collapses. It is the single drop of poison that makes the waters all undrinkable. That is why revenge is wrong. We simply cannot embark on the spiritual path with vengeance on our mind.

Ignoring the slain Polonius, Hamlet now proceeds to chastise his mother for her hasty remarriage.

Hamlet Leave wringing of your hands. Peace, sit you down,
And let me wring your heart; for so I shall
If it be made of penetrable stuff,
If damned custom have not brazed[85] it so,
That it be proof and bulwark against sense.

Unbelievable words from Hamlet—after killing an innocent man and ridiculing him, he voices concern that his mother may have become insensitive! When we are bent on condemning others, we often forget to look at ourselves.

Queen What have I done, that thou dar'st wag thy tongue
In noise so rude against me?

Hamlet Such an act
That blurs the grace and blush of modesty,
Calls virtue hypocrite, takes off the rose
From the fair forehead of an innocent love
And sets a blister there, makes marriage vows
As false as dicers' oaths. Oh, such a deed
As from the body of contraction[86] plucks
The very soul, and sweet religion makes

---

85 **brazed** hardened like brass

86 **contraction** the making of contracts

A rhapsody[87] of words. Heaven's face does glow
O'er this solidity and compound mass[88]
With tristful visage, as against the doom,[89]
Is thought-sick at the act.

Queen Ay me, what act
That roars so loud and thunders in the index?[90]

Hamlet now embarks on a comparison between his father and uncle as a means to chastise his mother on her choice in marrying his uncle. Shakespeare highlights the issue of choice here because it is particularly relevant to the central theme of the play.

Hamlet Look here upon this picture, and on this,
The counterfeit presentment[91] of two brothers.
See what grace was seated on this brow;
Hyperion's curls, the front of Jove himself,
An eye like Mars, to threaten and command,
A station[92] like the herald Mercury
New-lighted on a heaven-kissing hill;
A combination and a form indeed
Where every god did seem to set his seal
To give the world assurance of a man.
This was your husband. Look you now what follows.
Here is your husband, like a mildewed ear
Blasting his wholesome brother. Have you eyes?
Could you on this fair mountain leave to feed
And batten[93] on this moor? Ha, have you eyes?
You cannot call it love; for at your age
The heyday[94] in the blood is tame, it's humble,

---

87 **rhapsody** a jumble or mixed collection

88 **this solidity and compound mass** the Earth

89 **the doom** Judgment Day

90 **index** table of contents, formerly placed at the beginning of a book

91 **counterfeit presentment** portraits

92 **station** stance, bearing

93 **batten** gorge

94 **heyday** excitement

And waits upon the judgment, and what judgment
Would step from this to this?

Hamlet accuses his mother of being blind in choosing to marry his uncle. Her blindness, however, is cultivated and stems from her need to secure worldly comforts and security as a means to hide from the profound.

The choices we make in life determine our fate, and we make awful choices if we base our decisions on wrong information. By bringing up the issue of choice, Shakespeare alerts us to the danger of surrounding ourselves with false information. If we refuse to accept the truth and delude ourselves by beautifying reality to create a false world, we will be making wrong decisions based on wrong information. This is the disaster we are facing.

Thus, it is crucial to face the profound and to accept reality for what it is. Otherwise we will be seriously hurting ourselves, much like a man deciding to walk off a cliff because he believes he can fly. If we do not face up to the profound, our choices in life will be disastrous, and the words of Hamlet to his mother, below, will then also apply to us:

Hamlet Sense sure you have,
Else could you not have motion; but sure that sense
Is apoplexed,[95] for madness would not err
Nor sense to ecstasy was ne'er so thrilled
But it reserved some quantity of choice
To serve in such a difference. What devil was't
That thus hath cozened[96] you at hoodman-blind?[97]
Eyes without feeling, feeling without sight,
Ears without hands or eyes, smelling sans[98] all,
Or but a sickly part of one true sense
Could not so mope.[99]

The thematic resonance on the question of madness intensifies again. If we refuse to see the truth, deliberately delude ourselves with a falsely

---

95 **apoplexed** paralyzed

96 **cozened** cheated

97 **hoodman-blind** blind man's bluff

98 **sans** without

99 **mope** be in a daze

beautified world, and then base our decisions in life on this fantasy we create, are we not mad? Here, Hamlet actually proclaims it worse than madness.

Hamlet Oh shame, where is thy blush?
Rebellious hell,
If thou canst mutine in a matron's bones,
To flaming youth let virtue be as wax
And melt in her own fire; proclaim no shame
When the compulsive ardour gives the charge,
Since frost itself as actively doth burn
And reason panders the will.

We certainly let reason pander the will if we base our choices in life on the falsely beautified world we create. We will end up wasting our lives on futile pursuits and distractions without ever addressing the real issues of our existence.

Hamlet, on the other hand, has the courage to face the profound and to accept truth, and should have taken the correct path in life. Unfortunately, he has made the serious error of not heeding his inner conscience. His condemnation of his mother's madness in choosing to marry Claudius is thus ironical because of his own madness in choosing revenge instead of the spiritual path. Hamlet, too, has been "cozened at hoodman-blind," taken in by the convention that justifies, and even applauds, vengeance. He has failed to listen to his inner conscience and, as a result, has also based his choice on wrong information.

Queen Oh Hamlet, speak no more.
Thou turn'st my eyes into my very soul,
And there I see such black and grained [100] spots
As will not leave their tinct. [101]

Hamlet Nay, but to live
In the rank sweat of an enseamed [102] bed,
Stewed in corruption, honeying and making love
Over the nasty sty!

---

100 **grained** fast-dyed, indelible

101 **tinct** colour

102 **enseamed** greasy

Queen Oh speak to me no more.
These words like daggers enter in my ears.
No more, sweet Hamlet.

Hamlet A murderer and a villain,
A slave that is not twentieth part the tithe[103]
Of your precedent lord, a vice[104] of kings,
A cutpurse of the empire and the rule,
That from a shelf the precious diadem stole
And put it in his pocket—

Queen No more.

Hamlet A king of shreds and patches—

Hamlet, engrossed in his mother's failings, persists in rebuking her despite her pleas to stop, completely forgetting his own failings, and completely forgetting he has just rashly killed an innocent man. Finally, the reappearance of the ghost ends his ranting.

Hamlet Save me and hover o'er me with your wings,
You heavenly guards! What would your gracious
figure?

Queen Alas, he's mad.

Hamlet Do you not come your tardy son to chide,
That, lapsed in time and passion, lets go by
Th' important acting of your dread command?
Oh say.

The reappearance of the ghost at this point in the play is significant. In a conventional revenge story, we would expect this episode at the end of the play. Instead, the ghost reappears not after the death of Claudius, when its quest for vengeance has been fulfilled, but after the death of Polonius, when Hamlet's own fate has been sealed. And significantly, the ghost does not appear again after this scene. It has a no role in what happens from now on, being totally unable to stem the tragic results of its call for revenge. Thus, in setting him on the path of vengeance, the ghost has effectively brought about Hamlet's demise.

---

103 **tithe** tenth part

104 **vice** a character (often the buffoon) in morality plays

There is an echo here of *Titus Andronicus* and its portrayal of the never-ending cycle of horror unleashed by vengeance. In a symbolic depiction of the perpetuation of revenge, the ghost reappears at the very point when the next cycle of vengeance has just been initiated through the killing of Polonius. The ghost began the first cycle of revenge and is present at the start of the next, only this time the cycle is directed back at Hamlet. And still the ghost continues to urge him to vengeance.

Ghost Do not forget. This visitation
Is but to whet thy almost blunted purpose.
But look, amazement on thy mother sits.
Oh step between her and her fighting soul.
Conceit[105] in weakest bodies strongest works.
Speak to her, Hamlet.

Here, we see that while the ghost is no enlightened being, he is also no monster and is concerned for the Queen. The harm he has caused Hamlet stems from an ignorance of the effects of seeking revenge, not from willful malicious intent. Hence, the real demon is the path of vengeance, rather than the ghost itself.

Hamlet How is it with you, lady?

Queen Alas, how is't with you,
That you do bend your eye on vacancy,
And with th'incorporal air do hold discourse?
Forth at your eyes your spirits wildly peep,
And, as the sleeping soldiers in th'alarm,
Your bedded hair, like life in excrements,[106]
Start up and stand an end.[107] Oh gentle son,
Upon the heat and flame of thy distemper
Sprinkle cool patience. Whereon do you look?

Hamlet On him, on him! Look you how pale he glares.
His form and cause conjoined, preaching to stones,

---

105 **conceit** imagination

106 **excrements** outgrowths

107 **an end** on end

Would make them capable.[108]
Do not look upon me,
Lest with this piteous action you convert
My stern effects. Then what I have to do
Will want true colour—tears perchance for blood.

We are reminded again that compassion and thoughts of revenge are incompatible. They rule each other out, just as the path of vengeance destroys the spiritual path.

Queen To whom do you speak this?

Hamlet Do you see nothing there?

Queen Nothing at all; yet all that is I see.

It is apt here to echo the words of Hamlet to Horatio: "There are more things in heaven and earth, Horatio, than are dreamt of in your philosophy." We should not illogically presume, like the Queen, that we can perceive everything around us. Our senses limit what we can perceive directly, and even with sophisticated scientific equipment, there is a limit to what we can detect.

Hamlet Nor did you nothing hear?

Queen No, nothing but ourselves.

Hamlet Why, look you there, look how it steals away.
My father, in his habit[109] as he lived!
Look where he goes even now out at the portal.

Queen This is the very coinage of your brain.
This bodiless creation ecstasy
Is very cunning in.

We often dismiss phenomena we cannot perceive as mere "coinage of the brain." While this is true at times, it is also possible that we simply lack the required perceptual ability. Thus it is unwise to prematurely dismiss mystical experiences—widely described by saints and mystics on the spiritual path—simply because we cannot experience them. Since certain attainments are required before we can open the door to this inner

---

108 **capable** receptive, sensitive

109 **habit** clothes

journey, we need to take the spiritual path ourselves before we can verify these mystical experiences.

While Hamlet's vision of the ghost hardly qualifies as a mystical experience, it is our dismissive attitude toward experiences of this kind that we must be wary of. Realizing his mother may use his madness as an excuse to avoid transforming herself for the better, Hamlet moves quickly to dispel such thoughts.

Hamlet Ecstasy?
My pulse as yours doth temperately keep time.
And makes as healthful music. It is not madness
That I have uttered. Bring me to the test,
And I the matter will re-word, which madness
Would gambol from.[110] Mother, for love of grace,
Lay not that flattering unction[111] to your soul,
That not your trespass but my madness speaks.
It will but skin and film the ulcerous place,
Whiles rank corruption, mining all within,
Infects unseen. Confess yourself to heaven,
Repent what's past, avoid what is to come;
And do not spread the compost[112] on the weeds
To make them ranker.

Shakespeare is aware of our tendency to regard those with deeper realizations beyond the mundane as being psychologically unsound. This way, we can justify not confronting the truth ourselves, and thus avoid having to reform our lives and our attitudes.

Queen Oh Hamlet, thou hast cleft my heart in twain.

Hamlet Oh throw away the worser part of it
And live the purer with the other half.
Good night. But go not to my uncle's bed.
Assume a virtue if you have it not.
That monster, custom, who all sense doth eat
Of habits devil,[113] is angel yet in this,

---

110 **gambol from** spring away from

111 **unction** ointment

112 **compost** manure

113 **of habits devil** acts like a devil in maintaining bad habits

That to the use[114] of actions fair and good
He likewise gives a frock or livery
That aptly is put on. Refrain tonight,
And that shall lend a kind of easiness
To the next abstinence, the next more easy;
For use almost can change the stamp of nature,
And either the devil or throw him out
With wondrous potency.

This is the way of the spiritual path. It is a path of *metanoia*, requiring eventually a complete transformation of our being. The means towards this transformation is a step-by-step modification of our attitude and perception. As the Buddha says: "Whatever one thinks about and ponders over often, one's mind gets a leaning in that way."

Hamlet For this same lord
I do repent; but heaven hath pleased it so,
To punish me with this and this with me,
That I must be their scourge and minister.
I will bestow him, and will answer well
The death I gave him. So, again, good night.
I must be cruel only to be kind.
Thus bad begins, and worse remains behind.

Here is an important question: Is this tragic turn of events really ordained by heaven, as Hamlet suggests? Or is it the result of his own unfortunate choice of path? While he certainly did not intend to kill Polonius, there is little reason to suppose the action was willed by heaven. Surely, heaven has no need to use him as scourge or minister. It is therefore presumptuous for Hamlet to think he is needed to administer justice.

Polonius died because the effects of vengeance cannot be contained purely to the intended target. It inevitably spreads its circle of pain and fire to engulf others innocently straying onto its vicious path Polonius simply happens to be the first victim; more will be drawn into this chasm of blood and destruction. In taking this path of vengeance, Hamlet has made himself the angel of death. This is not ordained by heaven; it is the

---

114 **use** practice

result of his tragic choice of path, a choice that submits to the convention that approves vengeance.

Hamlet	One word more, good lady.
Queen	What shall I do?

Hamlet reverts to sarcasm and continues to give vent to the anger and bitterness within him.

Hamlet
Not this, by no means, that I bid you do:
Let the bloat King tempt you again to bed,
Pinch wanton on your cheek, call you his mouse,
And let him, for a pair of reechy [115] kisses,
Or paddling in your neck with his damned fingers,
Make you to ravel [116] all this matter out
That I essentially am not in madness,
But mad in craft.' Twere good you let him know,
For who that's but a queen, fair, sober, wise,
Would from a paddock, [117] from a bat, a gib, [118]
Such dear concernings hide? Who would do so?
No, in despite of sense and secrecy,
Unpeg the basket on the house's top,
Let the birds fly, and like the famous ape,
To try conclusions, [119] in the basket creep,
And break your own neck down.

Queen
Be thou assured, if words be made of breath,
And breath of life, I have no life to breathe
What thou hast said to me.

Hamlet
I must to England, you know that?

---

115 **reechy** filthy

116 **ravel** unravel

117 **paddock** toad

118 **gib** tomcat

119 **to try conclusions** to test results (the ape experiments to see if he too, like the birds, can fly if he enters the cage and then jumps out)

Queen Alack,
I had forgot. 'Tis so concluded on.

Hamlet There's letters sealed, and my two schoolfellows,
Whom I will trust as I will adders fanged—
They bear the mandate, they must sweep my way
And marshal me to knavery. Let it work;
For 'tis the sport to have the engineer
Hoist with his own petard,[120] and't shall go hard
But I will delve one yard below their mines
And blow them at the moon. Oh, 'tis most sweet
When in one line two crafts directly meet.

This speech reinforces the fact that Polonius's death was not the will of heaven but the result of Hamlet taking the path of vengeance. Here, Hamlet almost gleefully plots the demise of his two former friends, who are not only innocent of his father's murder but are even unaware of it. Hamlet spares little thought over their innocence, so intent is he now in the role of the hellish avenger.

One thing emerges clearly from this scene: the awesome strength of Hamlet's character. In the face of disaster, having mistakenly killed the wrong man, he shows no sign of despairing and continues with the reproach of his mother. And then, after the ghost's appearance, he has the presence of mind to counter his mother's suggestion that he is mad, realizing that this will weaken his admonishment of her. Here is a man facing total disaster who nonetheless resolutely continues to plan his bitter course, even warning his mother against revealing his secrets to the King and anticipating the ruin of his two former friends. The problem with Hamlet is not his weakness nor, as suggested by Goethe, his tenderness of character burdened with something too heavy to bear. Hamlet is incredibly strong and difficult to rattle, to the point of being callous.

To re-emphasize what Hamlet has now become, Shakespeare has him ridicule once more the man he has accidentally slain.

---

120 **petard** bomb

Hamlet This man shall set me packing.
I'll lug the guts into the neighbour room.
Mother, good night indeed. This counsellor
Is now most still, most secret, and most grave,
Who was in life a foolish prating knave.
Come, sir, to draw toward an end with you.
Good night, mother.

Hamlet is now truly into the role of the fiery angel of doom, the dreaded avenger with whom we would well shudder to cross paths.

4

Act IV

Scene 1

After the killing of Polonius, the threads of Hamlet's world begin to unravel, and all the ill effects of his course of vengeance come rushing in at an alarming pace. The ghost no longer has a role. It has already done its worst and can no longer help avert the tragic consequences of setting Hamlet on this path of destruction.

The King enters with Rosencrantz and Guildenstern, eager to learn what has happened.

King There's matter in these sighs, these profound heaves,
You must translate. 'Tis fit we understand them.
Where is your son?

Queen Bestow this place on us a little while.

[*Exeunt Rosencrantz and Guildenstern*]

Ah, my good lord, what have I seen tonight!

King What, Gertrude, how does Hamlet?

Queen Mad as the sea and wind when both contend
Which is the mightier. In his lawless fit,
Behind the arras hearing something stir,
Whips out his rapier, cries 'A rat, a rat,'
And in this brainish apprehension[1] kills
The unseen good old man.

---

1 **brainish apprehension** state of delusion

King Oh heavy deed!
It had been so with us had we been there,
His liberty is full of threats to all—
To you yourself, to us, to everyone.

The King realizes the rapier was meant for him, but with Machiavellian skill, he masks his knowledge by generalizing the danger Hamlet poses and justifies sending him away.

King Alas, how shall this bloody deed be answered?
It will be laid to us, whose providence[2]
Should have kept short, restrained, and out of haunt[3]
This mad young man. But so much was our love,
We would not understand what was most fit,
But like the owner of a foul disease,
To keep it from divulging, let it feed
Even on the pith of life.

Ironically, the King still fails to understand what is most fit. The real disease is not his tolerance of Hamlet but his refusal to acknowledge the true state of his existence. Thus, he is still allowing the disease to run rampant without seeking a cure.

King Where is he gone?

Queen To draw apart the body he hath killed,
O'er whom his very madness, like some ore
Among a mineral of metals base,
Shows itself pure: he weeps for what is done.

This, of course, is a blatant lie. Hamlet did not show any such remorse. Not only did he not weep for the slain man, he even ridiculed him. By the Queen's conspicuous lie, Shakespeare presents us with a stark reminder of Hamlet's true behavior.

King Oh Gertrude, come away!
The sun no sooner shall the mountains touch
But we will ship him hence; and this vile deed
We must with all our majesty and skill
Both countenance and excuse.

---

2 **providence** foresight

3 **out of haunt** away from others

The King sends Rosencrantz and Guildenstern to seek out Hamlet and to bring Polonius's body to the chapel. He then considers how to minimize the harm to himself and the Queen.

King Come, Gertrude, we'll call up our wisest friends,
And let them know both what we mean to do
And what's untimely done. So, haply, slander,
Whose whisper o'er the world's diameter,
As level as the cannon to his blank,[4]
Transports his poisoned shot, may miss our name
And hit the woundless[5] air. Oh come away,
My soul is full of discord and dismay.

What the King leaves unsaid is that he will also be plotting Hamlet's demise.

---

4 **blank** target

5 **woundless** incapable of being wounded

Scene 2

If Shakespeare meant to portray Hamlet as a sensitive hero burdened with a task too great to bear, we would now expect to find him in a state of remorse and perhaps, as the Queen suggests, even weeping for the slain Polonius. Instead, we find him in a callously jovial mood, having indulged in the gruesome trick of hiding the body, and now he is ready to crack morbid jokes about it.

Hamlet Safely stowed.
But soft, what noise? Who calls on Hamlet? Oh, here they come!

[*Enter Rosencrantz and Guildenstern*]

Rosencrantz What have you done, my lord, with the dead body?

Hamlet Compounded it with dust, whereto 'tis kin.

Hamlet's macabre jokes over the dead body are grossly insensitive. Shakespeare means to ensure that we do not overlook or mistake Hamlet's callous taunts over the slain man in Act III. This is what Hamlet has become in taking on the role of the avenger—brutal and savage.

His remarks also continue the shock treatment, begun in Act II, designed to attack our denial of mortality. They also serve as a prelude to the coming graveyard scene in Act V.

Rosencrantz Tell us where 'tis, that we may take it thence and bear it to the chapel.

Hamlet Do not believe it.

Rosencrantz Believe what?

Hamlet That I can keep your counsel and not mine own. Besides, to be demanded of a sponge—What replication[6] should be made by the son of a king?

Rosencrantz Take you me for a sponge, my lord?

---

6 **replication** reply

Hamlet	Ay, sir, that soaks up the King's countenance,[7] his rewards, his authorities. But such officers do the King best service in the end: he keeps them, like an ape, in the corner of his jaw; first mouthed, to be last swallowed. When he needs what you have gleaned, it is but squeezing you and, sponge, you shall be dry again.

Hamlet's description well fits the characterization of Rosencrantz and Guildenstern as career men who have sold their destiny for materialistic rewards. They will be "betrayed" when the inescapable truth seizes them in the end.

Rosencrantz	I understand you not, my lord.
Hamlet	I am glad of it. A knavish speech sleeps in a foolish ear.
Rosencrantz	My lord, you must tell us where the body is and go with us to the King.
Hamlet	The body is with the King, but the King is not with the body.

This last line is another of Hamlet's enigmatic remarks that has puzzled critics for centuries. The meaning, however, is indicated by the theme of the play: The physical body, which inevitably ages and dies, is certainly with the King, but the King refuses to recognize this impermanent nature of his body, so his mind is "not with the body." He behaves as though he will live forever, ignoring the inevitability of death, even to the extent of murdering his own brother for mere materialistic ends. This statement by Hamlet is thus part of the thematic resonance on our tendency to avoid facing up to the profound.

Hamlet	The King is a thing—
Guildenstern	A thing, my lord?
Hamlet	Of nothing. Bring me to him.

Hamlet's remark provides another foretaste of the coming graveyard scene. In the end, the title of king, or any prestigious position, amounts to nothing.

---

7 **countenance** favor

Scene 3

Scene 3 opens with the King in discussion with other lords over the problem of Hamlet. Rosencrantz and Guildenstern arrive shortly, and after informing the King they have still not found the body, they bring Hamlet to face him.

King	Now, Hamlet, where's Polonius?
Hamlet	At supper.
King	At supper? Where?
Hamlet	Not where he eats, but where he is eaten. A certain convocation of politic[8] worms are e'en at him. Your worm is your only emperor for diet: we fat all creatures else to fat us, and we fat ourselves for maggots. Your fat king and your lean beggar is but variable service[9]—two dishes, but to one table. That's the end.
King	Alas, alas.

To emphasize Hamlet's transformation into the brutal avenger, Shakespeare has him continue to deride Polonius even after the old man is dead.

What he says about the nature of death, however, is true. Why then do we find his remarks so appalling? The reason is that we deem these thoughts unthinkable and shun them because we wish to hide from the inevitable. Shakespeare has simply found an original way to thrust these thoughts upon us.

Hamlet now expands upon the theme:

Hamlet	A man may fish with the worm that hath eat of a king, and eat of the fish that hath fed of that worm.
King	What dost thou mean by this?
Hamlet	Nothing but to show you how a king may go a progress[10] through the guts of a beggar.

8 **politic** shrewd

9 **variable service** different courses of a meal

10 **progress** royal journey

Hamlet finds another way of saying "the king is a thing of nothing." Our worldly aspirations and titles are ultimately worth nothing.

King Where is Polonius?

Hamlet In heaven. Send thither to see. If your messenger find him not there, seek him i'th'other place yourself.

He openly taunts the King, suggesting that he belongs in "the other place."

Hamlet But if indeed you find him not within this month, you shall nose him as you go up the stairs into the lobby.

Hamlet stays doggedly on the theme of death and decay—and we continue being subjected to Shakespeare's shock treatment.

King [*To some Attendants*] Go seek him there.

Hamlet He will stay till you come.

King Hamlet, this deed, for thine especial safety—
Which we do tender, [11] as we dearly grieve
For that which thou hast done—must send thee hence
With fiery quickness. Therefore prepare thyself.
The bark is ready, and the wind at help,
Th'associates tend, [12] and everything is bent
For England.

Hamlet For England?

King Ay, Hamlet.

Hamlet Good.

King So is it, if thou knew'st our purposes.

Hamlet I see a cherub that sees them.

Hamlet hints that he can see more into the real purposes than the King supposes, as well as that heaven is watching. Cherubim are angels blessed with knowledge and keenness of vision. Hamlet now ends with an acerbic taunt about the remarriage of his mother to his uncle.

---

11 **tender** regard with tenderness

12 **tend** await

Hamlet But come, for England. Farewell, dear mother.

King Thy loving father, Hamlet.

Hamlet My mother. Father and mother is man and wife, man and wife is one flesh; so my mother. Come, for England.
[*Exit*]

King Follow him at foot.[13] Tempt him with speed aboard.
Delay it not. I'll have him hence tonight.
Away! For everything is sealed and done
That else leans[14] on th'affair. Pray you make haste.

Now, after everyone leaves, the King finally voices his true feelings, and we learn of his real purpose in sending Hamlet to England.

King And England, if my love thou hold'st at aught—
As my great power thereof may give thee sense,
Since yet thy cicatrice[15] looks raw and red
After the Danish sword, and thy free awe
Pays homage to us—thou mayst not coldly set[16]
Our sovereign process,[17] which imports at full,
By letters conjuring to that effect,
The present[18] death of Hamlet. Do it, England;
For like the hectic[19] in my blood he rages,
And thou must cure me. Till I know 'tis done,
Howe'er my haps,[20] my joys were ne'er begun.

---

13 **at foot** at his heels, closely

14 **leans** depends, relates to

15 **cicatrice** scar

16 **coldly set** disregard, consider lightly

17 **process** command

18 **present** immediate

19 **hectic** chronic fever

20 **haps** fortune

Scene 4

Scene 4 takes us to Fortinbras and the marching Norwegian army. Fortinbras sends his captain to greet the Danish king and to seek assurance of the promised passage through his land. On the way, the captain meets Hamlet and informs him that they are marching against Poland.

Hamlet Goes it against the main[21] of Poland, sir,
Or for some frontier?

Captain Truly to speak, and with no addition,
We go to gain a little patch of ground
That hath in it no profit but the name.
To pay five ducats—five—I would not farm it;
Nor will it yield to Norway or the Pole
A ranker[22] rate should it be sold in fee.[23]

Hamlet Why, then the Polack never will defend it.

Captain Yes, it is already garrisoned.

Hamlet Two thousand souls and twenty thousand ducats
Will not debate the question of this straw!
This is th'impostume of much wealth and peace,
That inward breaks, and shows no cause without
Why the man dies. I humbly thank you, sir.

As Hamlet implies, here is the height of human folly. He likens it to an abscess (the impostume), full of corrupt matter, which will destroy the body when it bursts inward, yet all the while remaining hidden from view. We have again an intensification of the thematic resonance on the "vile phrase, beautified," where the rotten core is concealed beneath an artificial layering of false beauty.

This episode also serves as another focused allegorical scene on our propensity to pursue meaningless goals rather than face up to the profound. It is an echo of the clowns who indulge in irrelevant gags while ignoring the main plot. Only here, this perverse behavior has reached the horrifying intensity of sending thousands to die over nothing.

---

21 **main** main territory

22 **ranker** higher

23 **in fee** outright

It is also significant that this act of utter folly, in dispatching thousands of men to their death over a useless piece of land, now serves as the basis for Hamlet to rebuke himself for delaying his revenge. If Shakespeare means to show that Hamlet has genuine cause to chastise himself, he would have given Fortinbras a more noble reason to attack Poland. This would have been so easy. Yet Shakespeare chooses an act of unbelievable foolishness as a foil for Hamlet's last soliloquy.

Captain God buy you, sir. [*Exit*]

Rosencrantz Will't please you go, my lord?

Hamlet I'll be with you straight. Go a little before.

Alone again, Hamlet launches into his last long soliloquy:

Hamlet How all occasions do inform against me,
And spur my dull revenge! What is a man
If his chief good and market[24] of his time
Be but to sleep and feed? A beast, no more.
Sure he that made us with such large discourse,
Looking before and after, gave us not
That capability and godlike reason
To fust[25] in us unused.

Here is the ultimate irony. The neglect of one's ability to reason is what Fortinbras should be accused of. To doom twenty thousand men over a piece of useless land and inflict all the pain and sorrow of war merely to satisfy his own craving for self-glorification must be the very height of human stupidity. Here, in stark display, is the most appalling abuse of our ability to reason. Yet Hamlet fails to recognize the utter madness of Fortinbras's campaign and amazingly even uses the actions of Fortinbras as a basis to chide himself.

Hamlet Now whether it be
Bestial oblivion,[26] or some craven scruple

---

24 **market** profit

25 **fust** grow moldy

26 **oblivion** forgetfulness

Of thinking too precisely on th'event[27]—
A thought which, quartered, hath but one part wisdom
And ever three parts coward—I do not know
Why yet I live to say this thing's to do,
Sith I have cause, and will, and strength, and means
To do't.

Shakespeare, again, stresses that Hamlet himself is unsure why he delays his vengeance.

Hamlet Examples gross as earth exhort me,
Witness this army of such mass and charge,[28]
Led by a delicate and tender prince,
Whose spirit, with divine ambition puffed,
Makes mouths at[29] the invisible[30] event,
Exposing what is mortal and unsure
To all that fortune, death, and danger dare,
Even for an eggshell. Rightly to be great
Is not to stir without great argument,
But greatly to find quarrel in a straw
When honour's at the stake.

Honor and ambition are ideas often used to justify the most dubious of actions. Here it is the excuse for the horror of sending twenty thousand men to their death for no reason. "Honor" that is devoid of compassion and used as an article of self-glorification should rightly be condemned.

Hamlet How stand I then,
That have a father killed, a mother stained,
Excitements[31] of my reason and my blood,
And let all sleep, while to my shame I see
The imminent death of twenty thousand men
That, for a fantasy and trick of fame,

---

27 **event** outcome

28 **charge** expense

29 **makes mouths at** scorns at

30 **invisible** unforeseeable

31 **excitements** urgings

Go to their graves like beds, fight for a plot
Whereon the numbers cannot try the cause,
Which is not tomb enough and continent[32]
To hide the slain? Oh, from this time forth
My thoughts be bloody or be nothing worth.

Unbelievably, Hamlet considers the callous folly of destroying twenty thousand men merely for "fantasy and trick of fame" as a virtue that shames him. Shakespeare makes a crucial point: Hamlet has no reason to chide himself for his delay. His real problem is his failure to realize that his inner conscience is delaying him. Tragically, he urges himself on to bloody vengeance, using the most flawed reasoning that Shakespeare could devise, and thus slides deeper into the dark path of destruction.

---

32 **continent** container

Scene 5

Scene 5 returns us to the royal residence in Denmark where the Queen has just learned about Ophelia's madness.

Queen I will not speak with her.

Gentleman She is importunate,
Indeed distract. Her mood will needs be pitied.

Queen What would she have?

Gentleman She speaks much of her father, says she hears
There's tricks i'th'world, and hems, and beats her heart;
Spurns enviously at straws;[33] speaks things in doubt[34]
That carry but half sense. Her speech is nothing,
Yet the unshaped use of it doth move
The hearers to collection.[35] They yawn[36] at it,
And botch the words up fit to their own thoughts,
Which, as her winks and nods and gestures yield them,
Indeed would make one think there might be thought,
Though nothing sure, yet much unhappily.

Ophelia, the one hiding from the inevitable by tame submission to convention, has been hit with the full force of reality and has completely disintegrated because she is unprepared for it.

Even before the death of Polonius, Ophelia had withdrawn somewhat from reality by vainly trying to shield herself from the profound. Now she withdraws even further and completely loses touch with the real world. Although the consequences are dramatic, it is only her degree of withdrawal that has changed. The question we have to ask—and which Shakespeare poses—is whether we are not equally withdrawing from reality by refusing to face the truth?

Horatio 'Twere good she were spoken with, for she may strew
Dangerous conjectures in ill-breeding minds.

---

33 **straws** trifles

34 **in doubt** of dubious meaning

35 **to collection** to gather meaning

36 **yawn** gape

Queen Let her come in.
[*Aside*] To my sick soul, as sin's true nature is,
Each toy seems prologue to some great amiss.
So full of artless jealousy[37] is guilt,
It spills itself in fearing to be spilt.

The Queen is aware that her world—and Hamlet's—is steadily and inexorably disintegrating.

Ophelia Where is the beauteous Majesty of Denmark?

Queen How now, Ophelia?

Ophelia [*Sings*] How should I your true love know
From another one?
By his cockle hat[38] and staff
And his sandal shoon.[39]

Queen Alas, sweet lady, what imports this song?

Ophelia Say you? Nay, pray you mark.
[*Sings*] He is dead and gone, lady,
He is dead and gone,
At his head a grass-green turf,
At his heels a stone.
Oh ho!

Ophelia's songs obliquely reflect the reason for her madness. Here, the search for a lover is dramatically cut short by the intrusion of death, and its finality hits hard.

Queen Nay, but Ophelia—

Ophelia Pray you mark.
[*Sings*] White his shroud as the mountain snow—

[*Enter King*]

Queen Alas, look here, my lord.

---

37 **jealousy** suspicion

38 **cockle hat** a cockleshell on the hat was a pilgrim's emblem

39 **shoon** shoes

Ophelia [*Sings*] Larded[40] with sweet flowers
Which bewept to the grave did not go
With true love showers.

The word "not" in the second line runs counter to the expected sense and also violates the meter, but it is a deliberate insertion. It alludes to our aversion to considering death in any of our plans and aspirations.

King How do you, pretty lady?

Ophelia Well, good dild you.[41] They say the owl was a baker's daughter. Lord, we know what we are, but know not what we may be. God be at your table.

The "owl" and the "baker's daughter" allude to a folk tale in which Jesus asked for bread and a baker's daughter ensured he was not given too much. As a result, she was turned into an owl. In line with the play's theme, "we know what we are, but know not what we may be," refers to our ultimate transformation, the transformation at death.

King Conceit[42] upon her father.

Ophelia Pray let's have no words of this, but when they ask you what it means, say you this.
[Sings] Tomorrow is Saint Valentine's day,
All in the morning betime,
And I a maid at your window,
To be your Valentine.
Then up he rose, and donned his clothes,
And dupped[43] the chamber door,
Let in the maid that out a maid
Never departed more.

King Pretty Ophelia—

Ophelia Indeed, without an oath, I'll make an end on't.
By Gis and by Saint Charity,
Alack and fie for shame,

---

40 **larded** adorned

41 **good dild you** may God yield or reward you

42 **conceit** brooding

43 **dupped** opened

Young men will do't if they come to't—
By Cock, they are to blame.
Quoth she, 'Before you tumbled me,
You promised me to wed.'
He answers,
'So would I a done, by yonder sun,
And thou hadst not come to my bed.'

This curious juxtaposition in Ophelia's songs of the two seemingly disparate themes of death and a faithless lover has intrigued many critics and generated differing interpretations. What is Shakespeare's purpose here?

The mixture of themes is so striking that we have to accept it as deliberate. Shakespeare draws an analogy between the betrayal of a faithless lover and Ophelia's new and painful situation. She had placed her faith on the illusion that she can hide from the inevitable by meekly conforming to the mores of society. This faith has now been shattered. It had, all along, been akin to trusting a fickle lover, destined to abandon her in the end.

King How long hath she been thus?

Ophelia I hope all will be well. We must be patient. But I cannot choose but weep to think they would lay him i'th'cold ground. My brother shall know of it. And so I thank you for your good counsel. Come, my coach. Good night, ladies, good night. Sweet ladies, good night, good night.

King Follow her close; give her good watch, I pray you.

After Ophelia and Horatio leave, the King informs Gertrude that Laertes has secretly returned from France and is being goaded into action by rumors and "pestilent speeches." Shortly, a messenger enters and informs them that Laertes had raised a riotous rabble that is even now breaking down the door to the castle. Laertes soon enters and confronts the King.

Laertes Oh thou vile King,
Give me my father.

Queen Calmly, good Laertes.

Laertes That drop of blood that's calm proclaims me bastard,
Cries cuckold[44] to my father, brands the harlot
Even here between the chaste unsmirched brow
Of my true mother.

True to form, even in emotional turmoil, Laertes's focus is on how he and his family will appear to society. As we have seen, Laertes is a man whose main concern is reputation; he tailors his behavior to the approval of society. His words reflect this attitude even while he rants about avenging his father.

His words also reflect the fact that society basically approves of revenge. Yet, spiritually, revenge is the wrong action to take. Many of the approved norms of society are actually at variance with the spiritual path, which is why some Shakespearean plays are considered problematic. Plays like *All's Well That Ends Well* and *Measure for Measure* are deemed "problem plays" because the wrongdoer does not incur the appropriate punishment. This is at odds with the convention that the villain be dealt his just deserts. The imposition of justice, however, is not the purpose of the spiritual path. Saints and bodhisattvas never clamor for justice; their only concern, out of compassion, is to save all beings from suffering.

King What is the cause, Laertes,
That thy rebellion looks so giant-like?
Let him go, Gertrude. Do not fear our person.
There's such divinity doth hedge a king
That treason can but peep to what it would,
Acts little of his will.

This speech is incredible coming from Claudius since his own treason destroyed the former king. Here is a true Machiavellian manipulator who almost believes the false righteousness he manufactures for himself. Truly, in the words of Hamlet, "the body is with the King, but the King is not with the body." He simply refuses to acknowledge his own mortality.

King Tell me, Laertes,
Why thou art thus incensed. Let him go, Gertrude.
Speak, man.

Laertes Where is my father?

---

44 **cuckold** man whose wife has been unfaithful

King	Dead.
Queen	But not by him.
King	Let him demand his fill.
Laertes	How came he dead? I'll not be juggled with. To hell, allegiance! Vows to the blackest devil! Conscience and grace, to the profoundest pit! I dare damnation. To this point I stand, That both the worlds I give to negligence,[45] Let come what comes, only I'll be revenged Most throughly for my father.

Laertes is the very model of what Hamlet chided himself for not being: the fearsome avenger who sweeps to his revenge without hesitation and without "thinking too precisely on the event"; here, in fact, practically without thinking at all. Is this the proper mode of behavior?

Shakespeare immediately provides the answer. Laertes, in behaving thus, instantly becomes the tool of the very villain himself, Claudius, who manipulates him to his own destruction. There is little doubt that this is Shakespeare's intended message, for he reprises and expands on this very theme in his next tragedy, *Othello*. Obsessed with meting out justice and avenging his honor, Othello inadvertently becomes the plaything of the devil himself, Iago. In a similar vein, Laertes is now reduced to an instrument of Claudius:

King	Who shall stay you?
Laertes	My will, not all the world's. And for my means, I'll husband them so well, They shall go far with little.
King	Good Laertes, If you desire to know the certainty Of your dear father, is't writ in your revenge That, swoopstake,[46] you will draw both friend and foe, Winner and loser?

45 **both the worlds I give to negligence** I do not care of the consequences in this world or the next

46 **swoopstake** indiscriminately sweeping all up

Laertes None but his enemies.

King Will you know them then?

Laertes To his good friends thus wide I'll ope my arms,
And, like the kind life-rend'ring pelican,[47]
Repast them with my blood.

King Why, now you speak
Like a good child and a true gentleman.
That I am guiltless of your father's death
And am most sensibly in grief for it,
It shall as level to your judgment 'pear
As day does to your eye.

Claudius toys with Laertes, manipulating him to serve his own ends; Laertes, in readily embracing revenge, becomes a mere puppet of the King. Both Hamlet and Laertes have now taken on the role of avenger. In doing so, Hamlet engineers his own destruction, and now Laertes follows him unwittingly.

Laertes How now, what noise is that?

Now, as though circumstances are in league with Claudius's scheming, Ophelia enters in her state of madness to fuel Laertes's will for revenge.

Laertes Oh heat, dry up my brains! Tears seven times salt
Burn out the sense and virtue of mine eye.
By heaven, thy madness shall be paid with weight
Till our scale turn the beam.[48] Oh rose of May!
Dear maid, kind sister, sweet Ophelia!
Oh heavens, is't possible a young maid's wits
Should be as mortal as an old man's life?
Nature is fine in love, and where 'tis fine
It sends some precious instance of itself
After the thing it loves.

Here, in Ophelia, probably bedecked fantastically with straws and flowers, Shakespeare presents a brilliant imagery of our inability to face

---

47 **life-rend'ring pelican** thought to nourish its young with its own blood

48 **turn the beam** tilt the bar of the balance

reality and our propensity to hide from the profound. Ophelia creates a false world for herself; yet her madness, although more marked, actually mirrors our own. Like Ophelia, we also create a false perception of our world, one that beautifies its rotten core and conceals the truth from ourselves.

Ophelia [*Sings*] They bore him bare-faced on the bier,
And in his grave rained many a tear—
Fare you well, my dove.

Laertes Hadst thou thy wits and didst persuade revenge,
It could not move thus.

Ophelia You must sing a-down a-down, and you call him a-down-a. O, how the wheel becomes it! It is the false steward that stole his master's daughter.

Very much mixed in with her songs about death is the idea of betrayal. We are reminded that Ophelia's belief—that she can avoid the inevitable by conforming to the mores of society—had been cruelly crushed and her faith thoroughly betrayed.

Laertes This nothing's more than matter.

Through Laertes's words, Shakespeare underscores the importance of what Ophelia's madness represents: While Ophelia's perception may be nonsensical—and hence nothing of importance—this tendency to hide behind a deluded perception of reality has severe consequences. For it is our refusal to face reality—and our grasping, instead, to a false perception of the world—that is the root cause of evil. If we realize the truth, we will cease behaving like sheep, penned up and awaiting slaughter, fighting to graze the best patch of grass. In being false to ourselves—in not facing the truth—we end up being false to others.

Ophelia There's rosemary, that's for remembrance—pray you, love, remember. And there is pansies, that's for thoughts.

Laertes A document[49] in madness; thoughts and remembrance fitted.

---

49 **document** lesson

Ophelia There's fennel for you, and columbines. There's rue for you. And here's some for me. We may call it herb of grace a Sundays. You must wear your rue with a difference. There's a daisy. I would give you some violets, but they withered all when my father died. They say he made a good end.

Different flowers traditionally represent different sentiments, so the distribution of the flowers by Ophelia suggests a symbolical meaning for each of the recipients. Unfortunately, we no longer know the exact recipient of each type of flower, since this is not on the script. Nonetheless, one unmistakable symbolism remains clear, and Laertes comments on it:

Laertes Thought and affliction, passion, hell itself
She turns to favour[50] and to prettiness.

Laertes reiterates the motif now brilliantly depicted in Ophelia's madness—the artificial beautification of what is rotten inside. The distribution of flowers by Ophelia builds on the dramatic image as the flowers beautify the whole rotten situation. The thematic resonance on the "vile phrase, beautified" is relentless.

Ophelia [*Sings*] And will he not come again?
And will he not come again?
No, no, he is dead,
Go to thy death-bed,
He never will come again.

His beard was as white as snow,
All flaxen[51] was his poll.[52]
He is gone, he is gone,
And we cast away moan.
God a mercy on his soul.

And of all Christian souls. God buy you. [*Exit*]

---

50 **favour** charm

51 **flaxen** white

52 **poll** head

Ophelia's last song focuses again on death. Her inability to cope with death is the prime reason for her madness, and the sudden loss of her means to hide from it has devastated her.

Laertes Do you see this, oh God?

King Laertes, I must commune with your grief,
Or you deny me right. Go but apart,
Make choice of whom your wisest friends you will,
And they shall hear and judge 'twixt you and me.
If by direct or by collateral hand
They find us touched,[53] we will our kingdom give,
Our crown, our life, and all that we call ours
To you in satisfaction; but if not,
Be you content to lend your patience to us,
And we shall jointly labour with your soul
To give it due content.

Laertes Let this be so.
His means of death, his obscure funeral—
No trophy, sword, nor hatchment[54] o'er his bones,
No noble rite, nor formal ostentation[55]—
Cry to be heard, as 'twere from heaven to earth,
That I must call't in question.

King So you shall.
And where th'offence is, let the great axe fall.
I pray you go with me.

Laertes has fallen prey to Claudius's designs. He has fulfilled thoroughly what Hamlet wrongly chides himself to become—the unthinking avenger. Laertes is now like a beast that has allowed his "capability and godlike reason to fust in him unused." Ironically, Hamlet's desire to assume this same role of avenger is what made him the target of Laertes's revenge.

---

53 **touched** implicated, guilty

54 **hatchment** heraldic tablet with coat of arms

55 **ostentation** ceremony

Scene 6

In this scene, sailors deliver a letter from Hamlet to Horatio.

Horatio [*Reads the letter*] *Horatio, when thou shalt have overlooked*[56] *this, give these fellows some means to the King. They have letters for him. Ere we were two days old at sea, a pirate of very warlike appointment*[57] *gave us chase. Finding ourselves too slow of sail, we put on a compelled valour, and in the grapple I boarded them. On the instant they got clear of our ship, so I alone became their prisoner.*

This episode clearly indicates that Hamlet is neither cowardly nor indecisive, for he boldly boarded the pirate's ship in the sea battle. Thus, being "pigeon-livered" can hardly be the reason for his delay in exacting revenge.

Horatio continues with the letter:

Horatio *They have dealt with me like thieves of mercy. But they knew what they did: I am to do a good turn for them. Let the King have the letters I have sent, and repair thou to me with as much speed as thou wouldest fly death. I have words to speak in thine ear will make thee dumb; yet are they much too light for the bore*[58] *of the matter.*

Thus we learn that Hamlet will shortly return, and the final resolution draws near.

---

56 **overlooked** looked over, surveyed

57 **appointment** equipment

58 **bore** caliber, size

Scene 7

Scene 7 opens with the King and Laertes in dialogue. Having revealed to Laertes that Hamlet, who killed Polonius, has also been seeking his own life, the King explains his inability to act publicly against Hamlet because of the great affection the Queen and the public have for him.

Just as Claudius hints that further news would reveal the steps he has taken against Hamlet, messengers arrive with letters from Hamlet himself, effectively informing him that his treacherous plan has failed.

Messenger	These to your Majesty, this to the Queen.
King	From Hamlet! Who brought them?
Messenger	Sailors, my lord, they say. I saw them not. They were given me by Claudio. He received them Of him that brought them.
King	Laertes, you shall hear them. Leave us. [*Exit Messenger*] [*Reads*] *High and mighty, you shall know I am set naked on your kingdom. Tomorrow shall I beg leave to see your kingly eyes, when I shall, first asking your pardon, thereunto recount the occasion of my sudden and more strange return. Hamlet.* What should this mean? Are all the rest come back? Or is it some abuse,[59] and no such thing?
Laertes	Know you the hand?
King	'Tis Hamlet's character. 'Naked' And in a postscript here he says 'Alone.' Can you devise me?

The word "naked" may mean "destitute," but it also refers to the absence of the layers of beautification used to hide the truth. Hamlet

[59] **abuse** deception

indicates that he has removed these layers from himself and obliquely hints that he returns to bare the truth.

Laertes I am lost in it, my lord. But let him come.
It warms the very sickness in my heart
That I shall live and tell him to his teeth,
'Thus diest thou.'

King If it be so, Laertes—
As how should it be so, how otherwise?—
Will you be ruled by me?

Laertes Ay, my lord,
So you will not o'errule me to a peace.

King To thine own peace. If he be now returned,
As checking at[60] his voyage, and that he means
No more to undertake it, I will work him
To an exploit, now ripe in my device,
Under the which he shall not choose but fall;
And for his death no wind of blame shall breathe,
But even his mother shall uncharge the practice
And call it accident.

Claudius now openly plots with Laertes; it is a measure of how much Laertes has degenerated into the role of the unthinking avenger that he no longer questions why the King is resorting to such deviousness.

Laertes My lord, I will be ruled,
The rather if you could devise it so
That I might be the organ.

King It falls right.
You have been talked of since your travel much,
And that in Hamlet's hearing, for a quality
Wherein they say you shine. Your sum of parts
Did not together pluck such envy from him
As did that one, and that, in my regard,
Of the unworthiest siege.[61]

---

60 **checking at** turning from

61 **siege** status

Laertes What part is that, my lord?

King A very riband in the cap of youth—
Yet needful too; for youth no less becomes
The light and careless livery that it wears
Than settled age his sables and his weeds[62]
Importing health and graveness. Two months since
Here was a gentleman of Normandy—
I have seen myself, and served against, the French,
And they can well on horseback, but this gallant
Had witchcraft in't. He grew unto his seat,
And to such wondrous doing brought his horse
As had he been incorpsed and demi-natured
With the brave beast. So far he topped my thought
That I in forgery[63] of shapes and tricks
Come short of what he did.

The image of the hobby-horse from Act III, Scene 2 appears again—a being half-man half-beast. Here, Shakespeare uses it to parody the behavior of Laertes who, in succumbing to the blind fury of revenge, has effectively allowed "that capability and godlike reason to fust in him unused." Following the words of Hamlet, he is effectively behaving as "a beast, no more."

After identifying the horse rider as Lamond, a friend of Laertes, the King relates how Lamond had praised Laertes's skill at the rapier, and how this has aroused Hamlet's desire to match skills with him. With Machiavellian skill, the King then incites Laertes to his revenge.

King Laertes, was your father dear to you?
Or are you like the painting of a sorrow,
A face without a heart?

Laertes Why ask you this?

King Not that I think you did not love your father,
But that I know love is begun by time,

---

62 **weeds** attire

63 **forgery** invention

And that I see, in passages of proof,[64]
Time qualifies[65] the spark and fire of it.
There lives within the very flame of love
A kind of wick or snuff[66] that will abate it;
And nothing is at a like goodness still;
For goodness, growing to a pleurisy,[67]
Dies in his own too-much. That we would do,
We should do when we would: for this 'would' changes
And hath abatements and delays as many
As there are tongues, are hands, are accidents,
And then this 'should' is like a spendthrift sigh
That hurts by easing.

The question of the delay is raised again. Is Hamlet wrong to delay? Should he act as the King now incites Laertes to do? Laertes's behavior, resembling that of an unthinking beast, can hardly be exemplary, as his answer to the King's next question demonstrates:

King But to the quick of th'ulcer;[68]
Hamlet comes back; what would you undertake
To show yourself your father's son in deed
More than in words?

Laertes To cut his throat i'th'church.

His reply is chilling, fit for the mind of the hellish avenger. The speed at which Laertes has descended to this brutal state contrasts greatly with that of Hamlet, marking Hamlet as the better man for withstanding the assault to his sensitivity and morality for so long. Nonetheless, with Laertes, Hamlet has also been transformed this way. This is the nature of revenge.

The King continues manipulating his unwitting instrument for evil:

---

64 **passages of proof** actual or proven cases

65 **qualifies** moderates

66 **snuff** burnt part of wick

67 **pleurisy** excess

68 **quick of th'ulcer** most sensitive part of the ulcer, i.e. heart of the matter

King No place indeed should murder sanctuarize;[69]
Revenge should have no bounds. But good Laertes,
Will you do this, keep close within your chamber;
Hamlet, returned, shall know you are come home;
We'll put on those shall praise your excellence,
And set a double varnish on the fame
The Frenchman gave you; bring you, in fine, together,
And wager o'er your heads. He, being remiss,
Most generous, and free from all contriving,
Will not peruse the foils, so that with ease—
Or with a little shuffling—you may choose
A sword unbated,[70] and in a pass of practice[71]
Requite him for your father.

Laertes I will do't.
And for that purpose, I'll anoint my sword.
I bought an unction of a mountebank[72]
So mortal that but dip a knife in it,
Where it draws blood, no cataplasm[73] so rare,
Collected from all simples[74] that have virtue
Under the moon, can save the thing from death
That is but scratched withal. I'll touch my point
With this contagion, that if I gall him slightly,
It may be death.

Not only does Laertes fall into step with the schemes of Claudius, he adds his own venom as well. The King decides that he will also prepare a cup of poison for Hamlet to drink during the bout, to ensure their plot does not fail.

In the midst of their scheming, the Queen, clearly distressed, rushes in.

Queen One woe doth tread upon another's heel,
So fast they follow. Your sister's drowned, Laertes.

---

69 **sanctuarize** protect

70 **unbated** not blunted

71 **pass of practice** thrust of treachery

72 **mountebank** traveling medicine seller

73 **cataplasm** medicated dressing, poultice

74 **simples** medicinal herbs

Laertes Drowned? Oh, where?

Queen There is a willow grows aslant the brook
That shows his hoary[75] leaves in the glassy stream.
There with fantastic garlands did she come
Of crow-flowers, nettles, daisies, and long purples,
That liberal[76] shepherds give a grosser name,
But our cold maids do dead men's fingers call them.
There on the pendent boughs her coronet weeds
Clamb'ring to hang, an envious sliver broke,
When down her weedy trophies and herself
Fell in the weeping brook. Her clothes spread wide,
And mermaid-like awhile they bore her up,
Which time she chanted snatches of old tunes,
As one incapable[77] of her own distress,
Or like a creature native and indued[78]
Unto that element. But long it could not be
Till that her garments, heavy with their drink,
Pulled the poor wretch from her melodious lay
To muddy death.

With the drowning of Ophelia, Shakespeare provides a brilliant imagery of our own state of denial. Even as she is sinking into the muddy waters, Ophelia refuses to recognize the truth of her situation; instead, she continues singing blissfully. This is a striking analogy to our own continued blissful denial that we are all in the process of dying, that every day brings us one day closer to death. In a cultivated state of ignorance designed to beautify the stark reality, we indulge in mundane pleasures and petty pursuits, even while we are inexorably sinking beneath the waters. If Ophelia is mad, so are we, and our vain attempt to live in our fantasized world will not hold us up anymore than the muddy waters can keep Ophelia afloat.

Laertes Alas, then she is drowned.

---

75 **hoary** silver-gray

76 **liberal** freely speaking

77 **incapable** unaware

78 **indued** adapted

Queen Drowned, drowned.

Laertes Too much of water hast thou, poor Ophelia,
And therefore I forbid my tears. But yet
It is our trick;[79] nature her custom holds,
Let shame say what it will. [*Weeps*] When these are gone,
The woman[80] will be out. Adieu, my lord,
I have a speech o'fire that fain would blaze
But that this folly douts it. [*Exit*]

King Let's follow, Gertrude.
How much I had to do to calm his rage.
Now fear I this will give it start again.
Therefore, let's follow.

Even with the tragic news of Ophelia's drowning, the King continues lying and manipulating. Here is the mind of a true criminal. His level of delusion and denial far exceeds that of the average man. One danger in denying the truths before us is that we, like Laertes, become prone to the manipulations of just such forces of evil.

---

79 **trick** disposition

80 **woman** womanly traits

5

Act V

Scene 1

Often in the works of Shakespeare, the scenes that do not move the main action along hold the key to the meaning of the play. In *Hamlet*, the famous graveyard scene fits this role and is yet another deliberately crafted focused allegorical scene.

Nearing the finale, Shakespeare employs an entire long scene to thrust home the meaning of the play. Both the central themes are presented with renewed intensity: the need to face up to the inevitability of death and the danger of taking a path of vengeance.

The scene opens with two grave-diggers preparing a grave.

Grave-digger Is she to be buried in Christian burial, when she willfully seeks her own salvation?

The grave-digger returns us to the question of whether technical considerations determine our afterlife. This echoes the problem we faced in Act III when Hamlet refrained from killing Claudius because of the belief that his praying automatically qualified him for heaven.

Other I tell thee she is, therefore make her grave straight.[1] The crowner[2] hath sat on her and finds it Christian burial.

Grave-digger How can that be, unless she drowned herself in her own defence?

Other Why, 'tis found so.

---

1 **straight** immediately

2 **crowner** coroner

It is a ridiculous presumption that a worldly court of law can determine one's fate in the afterlife. Shakespeare justly proceeds to make a grand mockery of this.

Grave-digger It must be se offendendo, it cannot be else. For here lies the point: if I drown myself wittingly, it argues an act, and an act hath three branches—it is to act, to do, to perform. Argal,[3] she drowned herself wittingly.

Shakespeare toys with the technical language of the court. "Se offendendo" is a play on the word "se-defendendo" which means "in self-defense."

Other Nay, but hear you, Goodman Delver—

Grave-digger Give me leave. Here lies the water: good. Here stands the man: good. If the man go to this water and drown himself, it is, will he nill he,[4] he goes, mark you that. But if the water come to him and drown him, he drowns not himself. Argal, he that is not guilty of his own death shortens not his own life.

Other But is this law?

Grave-digger Ay, marry is't, crowner's quest law.

Other Will you ha' the truth on't? If this had not been a gentlewoman, she should have been buried out o' Christian burial.

Grave-digger Why, there thou say'st. And the more pity that great folk should have countenance[5] in this world to drown or hang themselves more than their even-Christian.

His conclusion is appropriate, highlighting the ridiculousness of having a person's fate in the afterlife decided in a court of law. The problem, though, goes much deeper, for it is decidedly unclear whether or not Ophelia actually committed suicide.

---

3 **argal** blunder for "ergo" (therefore)

4 **will he nill he** whether he will or not

5 **countenance** privilege

Being too deluded to make rational decisions, can Ophelia even be judged guilty of suicide? And aren't all who commit suicide, to some extent, mad anyway? Since such unclear situations do exist, how can the mere technical point of suicide determine one's fate in the afterlife, especially if this fate is deemed eternal? In dubious cases like Ophelia's, we must then conclude that our eternal fate hangs on minor technical details.

This belief appears ridiculous, and that is exactly Shakespeare's point. Can technicalities like our nominal religion or the circumstances of our death, all by themselves, determine our eternal fate? We can always find cases in which these technicalities are unclear. Are we then to conclude that our eternal destiny revolves around fine details like those employed in a closely contested argument of law?

Shakespeare now presents us with three reminders of the nature of death. They are reminders because, although we may not wish to acknowledge them clearly, we already know them.

Grave-digger Come, my spade. There is no ancient gentlemen but gardeners, ditchers, and grave-makers—they hold up Adam's profession.

Other Was he a gentleman?

Grave-digger He was the first that ever bore arms.

Other Why, he had none.

Grave-digger What, art a heathen? How dost thou understand the scripture? The scripture says Adam digged. Could he dig without arms?

This part of the grave-digger's conversation is a play on the traditional doggerel:

"When Adam delved and Eve span.
Who was then the gentleman?"

The grave-diggers' words remind us that grave-diggers, and hence, death, have been with us since the time of Adam.

Grave-digger I'll put another question to thee. If thou answerest me not to the purpose, confess thyself—

Other Go to.

Grave-digger What is he that builds stronger than either the mason, the shipwright, or the carpenter?

Other The gallows-maker, for that frame outlives a thousand tenants.

Shakespeare provides a second reminder: life is impermanent. It is fleeting in nature, and, like the gallows, most physical structures will outlive us. Now comes a third reminder.

Grave-digger I like thy wit well in good faith, the gallows does well. But how does it well? It does well to those that do ill. Now, thou dost ill to say the gallows is built stronger than the church. Argal, the gallows may do well to thee. To't again, come.

Other Who builds stronger than a mason, a shipwright, or a carpenter?

Grave-digger Ay, tell me that and unyoke.[6]

Other Marry, now I can tell.

Grave-digger To't.

Other Mass, I cannot tell.

Grave-digger Cudgel thy brains no more about it, for your dull ass will not mend his pace with beating. And when you are asked this question next, say, 'a grave-maker.' The houses he makes lasts till doomsday.

This reminds us that we will not be returning to the mundane things we leave behind when we die. Death brings all that to a final end. We inevitably lose all the materialistic possessions and petty social benefits we struggle to accumulate.

The first grave-digger now sends his companion to buy liquor. He is singing and digging when Hamlet and Horatio appear on the scene.

---

6 **unyoke** end the day's work

Grave-digger [*Sings*] In youth when I did love, did love,
Me thought it was very sweet:
To contract-Oh-the time for-a-my behove,
Oh methought there was nothing meet.

Hamlet Has this fellow no feeling of his business that he sings at grave-making?

Horatio Custom hath made it in him a property of easiness.

Hamlet 'Tis e'en so, the hand of little employment hath the daintier sense.

Grave-digger [*Sings*] But age with his stealing steps
Hath clawed me in his clutch,
And hath shipped me intil the land,
As if I had never been such.

Even the song of the grave-digger holds an unmistakable message. It is about the inevitability of ageing and, eventually, death. Our carefree youth is quickly stolen by the inexorable march of time, and we end up being returned to the land.

The grave-digger now throws up a skull, and this moves Hamlet onto a philosophical discourse.

Hamlet That skull had a tongue in it, and could sing once. How the knave jowls[7] it to the ground, as if 'twere Cain's jawbone, that did the first murder! This might be the pate of a politician which this ass now o'er-reaches,[8] one that would circumvent God,[9] might it not?

Horatio It might, my lord.

Regardless of our abilities and power in life, it is all rendered useless at death, symbolized here by the bodily remains being irreverently tossed around by the grave-digger.

---

7 **jowls** hurls

8 **o'er-reaches** has the better of

9 **circumvent God** bypass the laws of God

Also, the mention of Cain echoes the plot. Like Claudius, Cain did not merely commit murder—traditionally, using the jawbone of an ass—but fratricide.

Hamlet Or of a courtier, which could say, 'Good morrow, sweet lord. How dost thou, sweet lord?' This might be my Lord Such-a-one, that praised my Lord Such-a-one's horse when he meant to beg it, might it not?

Horatio Ay, my lord.

Hamlet Why, e'en so, and now my Lady Worm's, chopless,[10] and knocked about the mazzard[11] with a sexton's spade. Here's fine revolution and we had the trick to see't. Did these bones cost no more the breeding but to play at loggets[12] with 'em? Mine ache to think on't.

Our problem is that we lack the trick to see this "fine revolution," as Hamlet puts it; and Shakespeare is intent on reminding us of our denial of the inevitable. His purpose, though, is not for us to despair over the hopelessness of our situation but to question whether it really is hopeless.

Unfortunately, contemporary mainstream science is unable to help us here because of its illogical insistence on leaving mind and consciousness out of the domain of science. Contemporary science relegates mind and consciousness to secondary, and hence inconsequential, phenomena. This flawed conclusion is ultimately based on an illogical argument: that since machines—i.e., scientific equipment—cannot detect consciousness, it does not "scientifically" exist.

To address this question, we have to fall back on the use of our own mind and consciousness as a probe. And this, essentially, is the mode of the spiritual quest. Here lies the purpose of Shakespeare in encouraging us to face up to the profound. If we remain too engrossed with the mundane world through our refusal to accept the inevitability of death, we may not heed the spiritual path before each and every one of us.

---

10 **chopless** without the lower jaw

11 **mazzard** head

12 **loggets** a game where blocks of wood are thrown at a stake

Grave-digger [*Sings*] A pickaxe and a spade, a spade,
For and a shrouding-sheet,
O a pit of clay for to be made
For such a guest is meet.

The grave-digger now throws up another skull.

Hamlet There's another. Why may not that be the skull of a lawyer? Where be his quiddities [13] now, his quillities, [14] his cases, his tenures, [15] and his tricks? Why does he suffer this rude knave now to knock him about the sconce [16] with a dirty shovel, and will not tell him of his action of battery? Hum! This fellow might be in's time a great buyer of land, with his statutes, [17] his recognizances, [18] his fines, his double vouchers, his recoveries. Is this the fine of his fines, and the recovery of his recoveries, to have his fine pate full of fine dirt? Will his vouchers vouch him no more of his purchases, and double ones too, than the length and breadth of a pair of indentures? [19] The very conveyances [20] of his lands will hardly lie in this box, and must the inheritor himself have no more, ha?

Horatio Not a jot more, my lord.

Shakespeare's point is clear. Death makes a mockery of all our efforts at building mundane and materialistic achievements.

Hamlet Is not parchment made of sheepskins?

Horatio Ay, my lord, and of calves' skins too.

---

13 **quiddities** quibbles, subtle arguments

14 **quillities** fine distinctions

15 **tenures** real estate titles

16 **sconce** head

17 **statutes** securities, mortgages

18 **recognizances** bond recognizing a debt or a legal obligation

19 **indentures** contracts

20 **conveyances** documents for transferring land

Hamlet They are sheep and calves which seek out assurance in that.

Truly, we will be akin to sheep and calves if we seek assurances in materialistic goals. All of it will come to naught and be meaningless when we die.

Hamlet I will speak to this fellow. Whose grave's this, sirrah?

Grave-digger Mine, sir.
[*Sings*] Oh a pit of clay for to be made
For such a guest is meet

Hamlet I think it be thine indeed, for thou liest in't.

Grave-digger You lie out on't, sir, and therefore 'tis not yours. For my part, I do not lie in't, and yet it is mine.

Hamlet Thou dost lie in't, to be in't and say 'tis thine. 'Tis for the dead, not for the quick:[21] therefore thou liest.

Grave-digger 'Tis a quick lie, sir, 'twill away again from me to you.

Hamlet What man dost thou dig it for?

Grave-digger For no man, sir.

Hamlet What woman then?

Grave-digger For none neither.

Hamlet Who is to be buried in't?

Grave-digger One that was a woman, sir; but rest her soul, she's dead.

As well as entertaining us with witty word play, this exchange revolves around the question of identity. Are we the same person when we die? Do we carry this same identity with us even beyond the grave, this "self" that we are so concerned about? This is a deep spiritual question which we will, sooner or later, have to contend with on the spiritual path.

The conversation now interpolates the events of Hamlet's life with the specter of death, giving the sense of his life as a process of marking time until the inevitable.

---

21 **the quick** the living

Hamlet How long hast thou been a grave-maker?

Grave-digger Of all the days i'th'year I came to't that day that our last King Hamlet o'ercame Fortinbras.

Hamlet How long is that since?

Grave-digger Cannot you tell that? Every fool can tell that. It was the very day that young Hamlet was born—he that is mad and sent into England.

Hamlet Ay, marry. Why was he sent into England?

Grave-digger Why, because he was mad. He shall recover his wits there. Or if he do not, 'tis no great matter there.

Hamlet Why?

Grave-digger 'Twill not be seen in him there. There the men are as mad as he.

Shakespeare obviously designs this joke for the English audience. The preceding dialogue, however, has a more serious role. The ominous revelation that the grave-digger commenced his work on the day of Hamlet's birth effectually begins a sequence that brings the reality of death ever nearer to Hamlet, like the sound of distant drumbeats incessantly drawing closer and closer.

Hamlet How came he mad?

Grave-digger Very strangely, they say.

Hamlet How strangely?

Grave-digger Faith, e'en with losing his wits.

Hamlet Upon what ground?

Grave-digger Why, here in Denmark. I have been sexton here, man and boy, thirty years.

The grave-digger twists the meaning of "ground" to that of the earth, together with a reminder of his profession as grave-digger. And Hamlet takes up the cue.

Hamlet How long will a man lie i'th'earth ere he rot?

Grave-digger Faith, if he be not rotten before he die—as we have many pocky corses nowadays that will scarce hold the laying in—he will last you some eight year or nine year. A tanner will last you nine year.

Hamlet Why he more than another?

Grave-digger Why, sir, his hide is so tanned with his trade that he will keep out water a great while, and your water is a sore decayer of your whoreson dead body. Here's a skull now hath lien you i'th'earth three and twenty years.

The drumbeats echoing the reality of death now draw closer to Hamlet:

Hamlet Whose was it?

Grave-digger A whoreson mad fellow's it was. Whose do you think it was?

Hamlet Nay, I know not.

Grave-digger A pestilence on him for a mad rogue! He poured a flagon of Rhenish on my head once. This same skull, sir, was Yorick's skull, the King's jester.

Hamlet This?

Taking the skull, Hamlet now holds in his hand the symbol of death, a symbol that belongs to a close companion from his childhood.

Grave-digger E'en that.

Hamlet Alas, poor Yorick! I knew him, Horatio; a fellow of infinite jest, of most excellent fancy. He hath borne me on his back a thousand times. And now, how abhorred in my imagination it is! My gorge rises at it. Here hung those lips that I have kissed I know not how oft. Where be your gibes now, your gambols, your songs, your flashes of merriment, that were wont to set the table on a roar? Not one now to mock your own grinning? Quite chop-fallen?[22] Now get you to

---

22 **chop-fallen** without the lower jaw

my lady's chamber and tell her, let her paint an inch thick, to this favour[23] she must come. Make her laugh at that.

We are confronted once again with the thematic resonance on the "vile phrase, beautified." All our mundane distractions in life can only serve as futile attempts at beautifying an unmistakably rotten situation. However thick we lay on the paint, we cannot hide from the profound in the end. In a poignant touch, Hamlet contemplates this truth as he gazes upon the skull of his intimate childhood companion.

Hamlet Prithee, Horatio, tell me one thing.

Horatio What's that, my lord?

Hamlet Dost thou think Alexander looked o' this fashion i'th'earth?

Horatio E'en so.

Hamlet And smelt so? Pah! [*Throws down the skull*]

Horatio E'en so, my lord.

Hamlet To what base uses we may return, Horatio! Why may not imagination trace the noble dust of Alexander till he find it stopping a bung-hole?

Horatio 'Twere to consider too curiously to consider so.

Horatio's words reflect our usual reaction; we have no wish to contemplate such an image, but it is exactly Shakespeare's aim to make us do so. Otherwise, we may waste our life pursuing worldly fame and riches that are ultimately meaningless. Even all the "glory" of Alexander could not help him in the end.

Among all the characters, Hamlet is the one with the courage to face the profound. He certainly does not consider it too curious to contemplate the reality of death.

Hamlet No, faith, not a jot, but to follow him thither with modesty enough,[24] and likelihood to lead it. Alexander

---

23 **favour** appearance

24 **with modesty enough** without exaggeration

died, Alexander was buried, Alexander returneth to dust, the dust is earth, of earth we make loam,[25] and why of that loam whereto he was converted might they not stop a beer-barrel?

Imperious Caesar, dead and turned to clay,
Might stop a hole to keep the wind away.
O that that earth which kept the world in awe
Should patch a wall t'expel the winter's flaw.[26]

Here is a third reference to Julius Caesar, a reminder yet again of the theme in Shakespeare's other play. Hamlet, with the courage to face the truth, should have open before him the door to the spiritual path. Tragically, he has instead fallen into the same trap as Brutus by failing to align himself with the Tao; he has failed to listen to his inner voice telling him revenge is wrong. This is the real tragedy of Hamlet.

And now the reality of death draws yet closer to him.

Hamlet But soft, but soft awhile.
Here comes the King,
The Queen, the courtiers.

The dialogue with the grave-digger is over, but the drumbeats echoing the reality of death are not silenced. Instead, they grow with dread intensity upon the arrival of the funeral procession which includes the King, Queen, Laertes, and the Priest.

Hamlet Who is this they follow?
And with such maimed[27] rites? This doth betoken
The corse they follow did with desp'rate hand
Fordo its own life. 'Twas of some estate.[28]
Couch we awhile and mark. [*Retiring with Horatio*]

Laertes What ceremony else?

Hamlet That is Laertes, a very noble youth. Mark.

Laertes What ceremony else?

---

25 **loam** mixture of clay, sand, straw, etc.

26 **flaw** squall

27 **maimed** incomplete

28 **estate** rank

Priest Her obsequies have been as far enlarged
As we have warranty. Her death was doubtful;[29]
And but that great command o'ersways the order,
She should in ground unsanctified have lodged
Till the last trumpet: for charitable prayers
Shards,[30] flints, and pebbles should be thrown on her.
Yet here she is allowed her virgin crants,[31]
Her maiden strewments,[32] and the bringing home
Of bell and burial.

Laertes Must there no more be done?

Priest No more be done.
We should profane the service of the dead
To sing sage requiem and such rest to her
As to peace-parted souls.

The Priest epitomizes blind adherence to dogma, to the extent of contravening the spiritual ideals of love and compassion. The audience would hardly feel that Laertes's rebuke is unwarranted:

Laertes Lay her i'th'earth,
And from her fair and unpolluted flesh
May violets spring. I tell thee, churlish priest,
A minist'ring angel shall my sister be
When thou liest howling.

Hamlet What, the fair Ophelia!

After confronting the reality of death concerning Yorick, his childhood companion, Hamlet now faces the terrible death of the girl he loved.

Queen [*She scatters flowers*] Sweets to the sweet. Farewell.
I hoped thou shouldst have been my Hamlet's wife:
I thought thy bride-bed to have decked, sweet maid,
And not have strewed thy grave.

---

29 **doubtful** suspicious

30 **shards** pieces of broken pottery

31 **crants** garland

32 **maiden strewments** i.e. strewn flowers

With horrible irony, these words reveal Polonius's mistake in compelling Ophelia to spurn Hamlet. There was no actual problem in their courtship, and Ophelia's rejection undoubtedly helped drive Hamlet into the role of the hellish avenger, something that ironically led to the demise of both Polonius and Ophelia.

Laertes Oh, treble woe
Fall ten times treble on that cursed head
Whose wicked deed thy most ingenious sense
Deprived thee of. Hold off the earth awhile,
Till I have caught her once more in mine arms.
[*Leaps in the grave*]
Now pile your dust upon the quick and dead,
Till of this flat a mountain you have made
To o'ertop old Pelion or the skyish head
Of blue Olympus.[33]

Hamlet What is he whose grief
Bears such an emphasis, whose phrase of sorrow
Conjures the wand'ring stars and makes them stand
Like wonder-wounded hearers? This is I,
Hamlet the Dane.

There is some dispute, at this point, whether Hamlet actually leaps into the grave. The First Quarto version of the play clearly states that "he leaps in after Laertes" while the Second Quarto and the Folio versions are both silent on this action. Some critics argue that it is unthinkable for Hamlet to couple his defiant confrontation with Laertes and Claudius with jumping into the grave as well. He would then seem too much the aggressor. However, in line with Hamlet's state of mind in soon challenging Laertes to a ranting match, it is almost certain that Shakespeare does intend to have him leap into the grave. Shakespeare is, in fact, making a point here.

Laertes [*Grappling with him*] The devil take thy soul!

[33] **Pelion, Olympus** mountains in Greece

Hamlet Thou pray'st not well.
I prithee take thy fingers from my throat,
For though I am not splenitive[34] and rash,
Yet have I in me something dangerous,
Which let thy wisdom fear. Hold off thy hand.

King Pluck them asunder.

Queen Hamlet! Hamlet!

All Gentlemen!

Horatio Good my lord, be quiet.

Hamlet Why, I will fight with him upon this theme
Until my eyelids will no longer wag.

Queen Oh my son, what theme?

Hamlet I loved Ophelia. Forty thousand brothers
Could not with all their quantity of love
Make up my sum. What wilt thou do for her?

King Oh, he is mad, Laertes.

Queen For love of God forbear him.

Hamlet 'Swounds, show me what thou't do.
Woo't weep, woo't fight, woo't fast, woo't tear thyself,
Woo't drink up eisel,[35] eat a crocodile?
I'll do't. Dost come here to whine,
To outface me with leaping in her grave?
Be buried quick with her, and so will I.
And if thou prate of mountains, let them throw
Millions of acres on us, till our ground,
Singeing his pate against the burning zone,[36]
Make Ossa[37] like a wart! Nay, and thou'lt mouth,
I'll rant as well as thou.

---

34 **splenitive** quick-tempered

35 **eisel** vinegar

36 **burning zone** sun's orbit

37 **Ossa** mountain in Greece

Hamlet's call for this ranting match is absurd and disturbing, although consistent with his rashness in leaping into the grave after Laertes. Why is Hamlet reacting this way? Also, his words, "Woo't weep, woo't fight, woo't fast," hardly amount to a poetic expression of deep love. Surely, Hamlet can do better than this. So what is Shakespeare's reason for Hamlet's behavior?

The point is this. In taking the path of the hellish avenger and in immersing himself for so long in a world of condemnation and vengeance, Hamlet has finally lost his finer sensitivity to the ideals of love. Upon witnessing Laertes's outpouring of grief, he is suddenly struck with the terrible realization of what he has lost. It is not only the loss of Ophelia, but also all that it represents of love and tenderness. So, in a frantic attempt to salvage something of value, Hamlet plunges into an emotional frenzy, leaps into the grave, grapples with Laertes, and rants about his love. But he remains a changed man, one who has taken the wrong route to a dark barren world, and it tragically shows.

Shakespeare thus reemphasizes a central message that has resonated throughout the play: The path of condemnation and vengeance is wrong. And he shows us why. Not only will it close the door to the spiritual path, it will ultimately destroy us.

Queen This is mere madness,
And thus awhile the fit will work on him.
Anon, as patient as the female dove
When that her golden couplets[38] are disclosed,[39]
His silence will sit drooping.

Hamlet Hear you, sir,
What is the reason that you use me thus?
I loved you ever. But it is no matter.
Let Hercules himself do what he may,
The cat will mew, and dog will have his day.

These closing lines of Hamlet have long posed an enigmatic riddle. The theme of the play, however, suggests it is Hamlet's distortion of perhaps a common saying at the time of Shakespeare, something like: "Do what one may, the cat will mew and dog will bark." Its transformation into

---

38 **golden couplets** pair of baby birds with yellow down

39 **disclosed** hatched

Hamlet's statement is typical of Shakespeare's artistry, for it says much with few words.

The statement reflects the entire theme of the play. Hamlet courageously faces the profound and realizes the inevitable; hence, he accepts "the cat will mew and dog will bark." But he has tragically coupled this realization and wrecked it with the mind of vengeance, reflected in the words that "dog will have his day." The statement is thus a terse summary of his state of mind and a reminder of the real tragedy that has befallen him.

King I pray thee, good Horatio, wait upon him.
[*To Laertes*] Strengthen your patience in our last night's speech;
We'll put the matter to the present push.[40]

In this penultimate scene, Shakespeare reiterates the two related central themes of the play. Through the King, he now informs us the climax has arrived.

---

40 **present push** immediate action

Scene 2

Shakespeare has crafted the final scene in *Hamlet* to encompass all the key elements of the play. This scene effectively summarizes the crucial points behind the play's message, and Shakespeare weaves these points into the action with the artistry of a master.

The scene opens with Hamlet informing Horatio about his discovery, during the sea voyage, of the King's plot against him. In the King's treachery, we encounter again the thematic resonance on how one ends up being false to others as a result of not being true to oneself. This is now interwoven with another thematic resonance that Shakespeare has crafted in the play: that of deception and counter-deception, which continues in sinister fashion.

Hamlet Sir, in my heart there was a kind of fighting
That would not let me sleep. Methought I lay
Worse than the mutines[41] in the bilboes.[42] Rashly—
And praised be rashness for it: let us know
Our indiscretion sometimes serves us well
When our deep plots do pall;[43] and that should teach us
There's a divinity that shapes our ends,
Rough-hew them how we will.

Horatio That is most certain.

Hamlet Up from my cabin,
My sea-gown scarfed about me, in the dark
Groped I to find out them; had my desire,
Fingered their packet, and in fine[44] withdrew
To mine own room again, making so bold,
My fears forgetting manners, to unseal
Their grand commission; where I found, Horatio—
Ah, royal knavery!—an exact command,

---

41 **mutines** mutineers

42 **bilboes** fetters

43 **pall** falter

44 **in fine** finally

Larded[45] with many several sorts of reasons
Importing Denmark's health, and England's too,
With ho! such bugs and goblins in my life,[46]
That on the supervise,[47] no leisure bated,[48]
No, not to stay the grinding of the axe,
My head should be struck off.

Horatio Is't possible?

Here is another echo of a recurring theme, concerning Hamlet's delay. By heeding his intuition, Hamlet discovers the plot against him, thus saving his life. And here is fine irony. Hamlet, throughout the play, has failed to listen to the same inner voice telling him revenge is wrong. It causes him to delay his actions, but he fails to discern clearly what it is, within himself, that causes him to delay. This failure is the real tragedy of Hamlet, for the path of vengeance has plunged him into a spiral of spiritual desecration and destruction.

Hamlet Here's the commission, read it at more leisure.
But wilt thou hear now how I did proceed?

Horatio I beseech you.

Hamlet Being thus benetted round with villainies—
Ere I could make a prologue to my brains,
They had begun the play—I sat me down,
Devised a new commission, wrote it fair—
I once did hold it, as our statists[49] do,
A baseness to write fair, and laboured much
How to forget that learning, but, sir, now
It did me yeoman's service.

This digression on "writing fair" jolts the flow of the narrative, much the same way as Hamlet's need in Act I to suddenly write down the idea that "one may smile, and smile, and be a villain." It is also similar to the

45 **larded** adorned

46 **bugs and goblins in my life** terrors (imagined) that would result if I was allowed to live

47 **supervise** reading

48 **no leisure bated** no time lost

49 **statists** statesmen

way Polonius remarks in Act II on the vileness of the phrase "beautified." The effect here, as before, is deliberate and for the same purpose.

Hamlet Wilt thou know
Th'effect of what I wrote?

Horatio Ay, good my lord.

Hamlet As earnest conjuration from the King,
As England was his faithful tributary,
As love between them like the palm might flourish,
As peace should still her wheaten garland wear
And stand a comma[50] 'tween their amities,
And many such-like 'as'es of great charge,[51]
That on the view and knowing of these contents,
Without debatement further more or less,
He should those bearers put to sudden death,
Not shriving-time[52] allowed.

The emphasis on the practice of writing "fair" thus echoes another recurring theme—that of beautifying what is rotten inside. Here, Hamlet's appalling message, sealing the doom of his former friends, is beautified by "fair" writing with "many such-like 'as'es" (a pun on "asses").

In addition, the bizarre pattern of deceit and falsehood continues unabated with Hamlet reciprocating the King's treachery with his own.

Horatio So Guildenstern and Rosencrantz go to't.

Hamlet Why, man, they did make love to this employment.
They are not near my conscience, their defeat
Does by their own insinuation[53] grow.
'Tis dangerous when the baser nature comes
Between the pass[54] and fell[55] incensed points
Of mighty opposites.

---

50 **comma** link

51 **charge** importance or burden

52 **shriving-time** time for confession and absolution

53 **insinuation** meddling

54 **pass** thrust

55 **fell** fierce

This speech brings up another major theme in the play—the transformation of Hamlet into the brutal avenger "roasted in wrath and fire." Hamlet has needlessly and mercilessly dispatched his two childhood friends to their doom. That they are ignorant of Claudius's plot does not bother Hamlet at all. The path of vengeance has made him cruel and remorseless, even to the extent of denying his former friends any "shriving time" before their death.

Now Shakespeare reminds us again of the crucial error that led Hamlet to this terrible path. Like Brutus, he has failed to listen to his inner voice, his deeper conscience, and has hence failed to abide by divine law and to flow with the Tao.

Horatio Why, what a king is this!

Hamlet Does it not, think thee, stand me now upon[56]—
He that hath killed my king and whored my mother,
Popped in between th'election[57] and my hopes,
Thrown out his angle[58] for my proper life
And with such cozenage[59]—is't not perfect conscience
To quit[60] him with this arm? And is't not to be damned
To let this canker of our nature come
In further evil?

Finally, Hamlet states the real reason for his delay, but only when it no longer affects him. The problem was his conscience all along. In all his soliloquies, Hamlet has failed to acknowledge his conscience, and we can now see the tragic result; the path of vengeance has made him cruelly brutal, capable of destroying his childhood friends without a hint of remorse.

Significantly, Horatio does not answer Hamlet's question.

Horatio It must be shortly known to him from England
What is the issue of the business there.

---

56 **stand me now upon** become incumbent upon me

57 **election** i.e. to being king

58 **angle** fishing hook

59 **cozenage** deception, trickery

60 **quit** repay

Hamlet It will be short. The interim is mine.
And a man's life's no more than to say 'one.'
But I am very sorry, good Horatio,
That to Laertes I forgot myself;
For by the image of the cause I see
The portraiture of his. I'll court his favours.
But sure the bravery of his grief did put me
Into a towering passion.

With fine Shakespearean irony, Hamlet declares his right to revenge, yet expects to gain forgiveness from Laertes and to turn him from a cause that is, in his own words, the image of his own. Perhaps there is a difference in that Claudius deliberately plots murder, while the killing of Polonius is an accident. Nonetheless, Hamlet deliberately and needlessly sends his two childhood friends to their doom. He is thus hardly in a position to claim a moral difference.

Horatio Peace, who comes here?

Shakespeare reiterates another recurring theme through the appearance of Osric, who fills the gap left by the departure of Polonius, Rosencrantz, and Guildenstern. Osric now portrays the shallowness of our mundane preoccupations in life, our alternative to facing up to the profound.

Osric Your lordship is right welcome back to Denmark.

Hamlet I humbly thank you sir. Dost know this water-fly?

Horatio No, my good lord.

Hamlet Thy state is the more gracious, for 'tis a vice to know him. He hath much land and fertile. Let a beast be lord of beasts and his crib shall stand at the king's mess.[61] 'Tis a chough,[62] but, as I say, spacious in the possession of dirt.

Osric Sweet lord, if your lordship were at leisure, I should impart a thing to you from his Majesty.

---

61 **mess** table

62 **chough** jackdaw

Hamlet I will receive it, sir, with all diligence of spirit. Put your bonnet to his right use: 'tis for the head.

Osric I thank your lordship, it is very hot.

With little patience for shallow mundane behavior, Hamlet proceeds to taunt Osric, much the same way he taunted Polonius earlier.

Hamlet No, believe me, 'tis very cold, the wind is northerly.

Osric It is indifferent cold, my lord, indeed.

Hamlet But yet methinks it is very sultry and hot for my complexion.[63]

Osric Exceedingly, my lord, it is very sultry—as 'twere—I cannot tell how. My lord, his Majesty bade me signify to you that he has laid a great wager on your head. Sir, this is the matter—

Hamlet [*Signing to him to put on his hat*] I beseech you remember—

Osric Nay, good my lord, for my ease, in good faith. Sir, here is newly come to court Laertes; believe me an absolute gentleman, full of most excellent differences,[64] of very soft society and great showing. Indeed, to speak feelingly of him, he is the card or calender[65] of gentry; for you shall find in him the continent[66] of what part a gentleman would see.

This speech is another display of artificial beautification, much like writing "fair." Here it also highlights how someone like Laertes—who avoids the profound but molds his behavior for the approval of society—will often be praised and emulated.

---

[63] **complexion** temperament

[64] **differences** distinguishing qualities

[65] **card or calendar** chart or guide

[66] **continent** containing or embodiment

Hamlet Sir, his definement[67] suffers no perdition[68] in you; though I know to divide him inventorially would dozy[69] th'arithmetic of memory, and, yet but yaw[70] neither, in respect of his quick sail. But, in the verity of extolment, I take him to be a soul of great article and his infusion[71] of such dearth[72] and rareness as, to make true diction of him, his semblable[73] is his mirror and who else would trace him his umbrage,[74] nothing more.

Hamlet takes up the challenge to outdo Osric in speaking "fair." The parody, however, is lost on Osric, who probably feels this kind of court dialogue is natural.

Osric Your lordship speaks most infallibly of him.

Hamlet The concernancy,[75] sir? Why do we wrap the gentleman in our more rawer breath?

Osric Sir?

Horatio Is't not possible to understand in another tongue? You will to't, sir, really.

Both Hamlet and Horatio urge Osric to get to the point. Horatio is telling him to stop speaking "fair" and to speak plainly, i.e., in "another tongue."

Hamlet What imports the nomination of this gentleman?

Osric Of Laertes?

Horatio His purse is empty already, all's golden words are spent.

---

67 **definement** description

68 **perdition** loss

69 **dozy** dizzy

70 **yaw** deviating erratically like a wildly steering ship

71 **infusion** essence, nature

72 **dearth** scarcity

73 **semblable** likeness or equal

74 **umbrage** shadow

75 **concernancy** relevance

Hamlet Of him, sir.

Osric I know you are not ignorant—

Hamlet I would you did, sir. Yet, in faith if you did, it would not much approve[76] me. Well, sir?

Incredibly, up till now, Osric has still said nothing of consequence. He really does outdo Polonius.

Osric You are not ignorant of what excellence Laertes is—

Hamlet I dare not confess that, lest I should compare with him in excellence; but to know a man well were to know himself.

Osric I mean, sir, for his weapon; but in the imputation[77] laid on him, by them in his meed,[78] he's unfellowed.

Hamlet What's his weapon?

Osric Rapier and dagger.

Hamlet That's two of his weapons. But well.

Finally, after prolonged meaningless oration, Osric begins the actual message. Still, he continues with as much "beautification" as before. The thematic resonance is relentless.

To move along the action of the play, a few lines of dialogue with Osric would have sufficed. Yet Shakespeare, at the play's critical point, chooses to dwell so long on the character of Osric and on how he beautifies and wastes time on irrelevancies. The dialogue with Osric is thus yet another focused allegorical scene deliberately crafted by Shakespeare to reemphasize this recurring theme.

Truly, Osric is an echo of the clowns who speak more than is set down for them to gain laughs while neglecting the point of the play. The question Shakespeare poses is whether or not we are also like this: Do we not indulge our lives chasing after irrelevancies while neglecting the main issue? Do

---

76 **approve** commend

77 **imputation** attribution, reputation

78 **meed** merit

we not beautify reality and hide from the truth by petty distractions? In other words, do we not see a reflection of Osric in ourselves?

Osric The King, sir, hath wagered with him six Barbary horses, against the which he has impawned,[79] as I take it, six French rapiers and poniards, with their assigns,[80] as girdle, hanger, and so. Three of the carriages, in faith, are very dear to fancy, very responsive to the hilts, most delicate carriages, and of very liberal conceit.

Hamlet What call you the carriages?

Horatio I knew you must be edified by the margin ere you had done.

Osric The carriages, sir, are the hangers.

Hamlet The phrase would be more germane to the matter if we could carry a cannon by our sides. I would it might be hangers till then. But on. Six Barbary horses against six French swords, their assigns, and three liberal-conceited carriages; that's the French bet against the Danish. Why is this—impawned, as you call it?

Osric The King, sir, hath laid, sir, that in a dozen passes between yourself and him he shall not exceed you three hits; he hath laid on twelve for nine. And it would come to immediate trial if your lordship would vouchsafe the answer.

At long last, the challenge is delivered. Hamlet accepts and Osric leaves to prepare for the duel. Before the arrival of the King, Queen, and Laertes, Horatio and Hamlet exchange significant words.

Horatio You will lose, my lord.

Hamlet I do not think so. Since he went into France, I have been in continual practice. I shall win at the odds.

---

79 **impawned** staked

80 **assigns** accompaniments

Thou wouldst not think how ill all's here about my heart; but it is no matter.

Horatio Nay, good my lord.

Hamlet It is but foolery, but it is such a kind of gaingiving[81] as would perhaps trouble a woman.

Hamlet has a premonition of impending disaster, but he chooses to ignore it. This echoes again a crucial point in the play, for Hamlet has previously ignored another intuitive impression—that of his inner voice telling him revenge is wrong. It has delayed his vengeance, but he has tragically failed to recognize the message clearly. Now he is making a similar mistake, and this time, it proves fatal.

Significantly, the one time that Hamlet does heed his intuitive sense—while en route for England—it saves his life. But now, in spite of Horatio's advice, he chooses again not to heed his inner prompting.

Horatio If your mind dislike anything, obey it. I will forestall their repair hither and say you are not fit.

Hamlet Not a whit. We defy augury. There is special providence in the fall of a sparrow. If it be now, 'tis not to come; if it be not to come, it will be now; if it be not now, yet it will come. The readiness is all. Since no man of aught he leaves, knows aught, what is't to leave betimes?[82] Let be.

These words highlight the characteristic of Hamlet most relevant to the message of the play. Among the characters, Hamlet is the one with the courage to confront the profound. He unflinchingly faces the inevitability of death. This courage to accept the truth is a necessary trait for the spiritual path, and thus Hamlet is most qualified to take it. Tragically he has, instead, taken the path of vengeance, a path of spiritual desecration. The characterization of Hamlet is thus an echo of his words: "Let Hercules himself do what he may, the cat will mew, and dog will have his day." While Hamlet courageously accepts the truth, he taints this pure mind with the bitterness of vengeance.

---

[81] **gaingiving** misgiving

[82] **betimes** early

What is needed in life is to prepare for the inevitable. In Hamlet's own words, "the readiness is all." This, however, means more than just accepting death; it means being prepared for what it leads to. It means being ready with an inner light to guide us to higher mystical heights, a light that senses the profound love and pervading oneness of the universe. Thus, although Hamlet is willing to face death, he is unfortunately not ready. Instead of preparing himself spiritually, he has transformed himself into the dreaded avenger, a role intent on cruelty.

The play now continues with the entrance of the King, Queen, Laertes, Osric, and all the state, together with attendants carrying foils and daggers. We have reached the climax of the play, and Shakespeare presents us with a dramatic combination of two of its recurring themes: that of being false to others as a result of being false to oneself; and that of artificially beautifying what is rotten inside.

We are about to witness a duel of utmost sinister and murderous intent. Yet it is cloaked under a layer of beautification to appear, before the whole court, as affable entertainment. The act of being false is thus perpetrated by artificial beautification. The King begins the charade with the ultimate gesture of hypocrisy:

King Come, Hamlet, come, and take this hand from me.
[*Puts Laertes's hand into Hamlet's*]

Hamlet Give me your pardon, sir. I have done you wrong;
But pardon't as you are a gentleman.
This presence[83] knows, and you must needs have heard,
How I am punished with a sore distraction.
What I have done
That might your nature, honour, and exception[84]
Roughly awake, I here proclaim was madness.
Was't Hamlet wronged Laertes? Never Hamlet.
If Hamlet from himself be ta'en away,
And when he's not himself does wrong Laertes,
Then Hamlet does it not, Hamlet denies it.

---

83 **presence** assembly

84 **exception** objection

Who does it then? His madness. If't be so,
Hamlet is of the faction that is wronged;
His madness is poor Hamlet's enemy.
Sir, in this audience,
Let my disclaiming from a purposed evil
Free me so far in your most generous thoughts
That I have shot my arrow o'er the house
And hurt my brother.

Shakespeare brings us back to the recurring question: Who actually is mad? In one sense, Hamlet is lying here, since his antic disposition is artificially put on. Yet at a deeper level, he may well be speaking the truth. His decision to take the path of vengeance, a path of spiritual desecration, is really an act of delusion stemming from ignorance of the deeper spiritual principles.

In that sense, anyone who wrongs others willfully may also be considered mad, for this too is an act of delusion based on ignorance and a refusal to accept reality. Thus Claudius can certainly be considered mad. Hamlet, however, is not about to forgive the King for his madness, even though he seeks pardon for his own.

Shakespeare, of course, also extends the question of sanity to all of us: When we refuse to face up to the truth and behave in total contradiction to reality, can we claim to be sane? When we spend our lives distracting ourselves in petty mundane matters in a futile attempt to escape the truth, are we not mad?

Laertes I am satisfied in nature,
Whose motive in this case should stir me most
To my revenge; but in my terms of honour
I stand aloof, and will no reconcilement
Till by some elder masters of known honour
I have a voice and precedent[85] of peace[86]
To keep my name ungored. But till that time
I do receive your offered love like love
And will not wrong it.

---

[85] **voice and precedent** firm statement justified by precedent

[86] **of peace** for reconciliation

If Hamlet is lying, so is Laertes. The bizarre dance of deception and counter-deception plays out again. Here is beautification in its most sinister expression, an outward charade concealing the intent of murder.

Even while participating in this deception, Laertes nonetheless speaks true to his character—one that tailors his behavior for the approval of society. He is concerned, as he puts it, to keep his name "ungored."

Hamlet I embrace it freely,
And will this brother's wager frankly play.
Give us the foils.

Laertes Come, one for me.

Hamlet I'll be your foil,[87] Laertes. In mine ignorance
Your skill shall be like a star i'th'darkest night.
Stick fiery off [88] indeed.

Laertes You mock me, sir.

Hamlet No, by this hand.

The intensity of the drama is palpable. This apparently friendly contest with its almost jovial banter actually veils the sinister intent of murder.

King Give them the foils, young Osric. Cousin Hamlet,
You know the wager?

Hamlet Very well, my lord.
Your Grace has laid the odds o'th'weaker side.

King I do not fear it. I have seen you both,
But since he is bettered, we have therefore odds.

Laertes This is too heavy. Let me see another.

Hamlet This likes me well. These foils have all a length?

Osric Ay, my good lord.

As the King predicted, Hamlet, with his trusting nature, fails to examine the foils. He prepares to play with Laertes, and the trap is sprung.

King Set me the stoups of wine upon the table.
If Hamlet give the first or second hit,

---

87 **foil** material used to display a jewel

88 **stick fiery off** be brilliant in contrast

Or quit[89] in answer of the third exchange,
Let all the battlements their ordnance fire;
The King shall drink to Hamlet's better breath,
And in the cup an union[90] shall he throw
Richer than that which four successive kings
In Denmark's crown have worn. Give me the cups—
And let the kettle[91] to the trumpet speak,
The trumpet to the cannoneer without,
The cannons to the heavens, the heavens to earth,
'Now the King drinks to Hamlet.' Come, begin.
And you, the judges, bear a wary eye.

The King, true to character, indulges in excesses of celebration and exaggerated displays. We are thus presented with an almost alarming depiction of "beautification," an extravagant charade concealing pure malevolence.

Hamlet Come on, sir.

Laertes Come, my lord.

They play their first bout, and Hamlet makes the first appeal.

Hamlet One!

Laertes No.

Hamlet Judgement.

Osric A hit, a very palpable hit.

Laertes Well, again.

The tension mounts as the facade continues. It still appears a friendly contest, but the beautification must inevitably break and the terrible truth spill out. This is the way of all artificial beautification of reality, including our own vain attempts at hiding from the profound. In the end, we will not escape, as Shakespeare points out with powerful and lasting imagery.

---

89 **quit** pays back, i.e. hits back

90 **union** high quality pearl

91 **kettle** kettle-drum

King Stay, give me drink. Hamlet this pearl is thine.
Here's to thy health.
[*Drums; trumpet; and shot goes off*]
Give him the cup.

Hamlet I'll play this bout first. Set it by awhile.
Come.

The King's attempt at poisoning Hamlet with the drink fails, so the charade continues yet. But the end is near. They play again and Hamlet makes another hit.

Hamlet Another hit. What say you?

Laertes A touch, a touch, I do confess.

King Our son shall win.

Queen He's fat and scant of breath.
Here, Hamlet, take my napkin, rub thy brows.
The Queen carouses to thy fortune, Hamlet.

Hamlet Good madam.

King Gertrude, do not drink.

Queen I will, my lord, I pray you pardon me.

The charade begins to crack, but not in the way the King planned. The Queen drinks from the fatal cup and offers it to Hamlet.

King [*Aside*] It is the poisoned cup. It is too late.

The King's evil goes awry, and he is punished with the incredible horror of having to watch helplessly while his loved one drinks his own poison. Ironically, he is unable to act physically to save the Queen, for he is trapped in his own charade.

Hamlet I dare not drink yet, madam; by and by.

Queen Come, let me wipe thy face.

Laertes My lord, I'll hit him now.

King I do not think't.

Laertes [*Aside*] And yet it is almost against my conscience.

For the first time since the death of Polonius, Laertes takes note of his conscience. Faced with the stark reality of the situation, and, for once, not obsessed with the approval of society, he is suddenly aware of the inner voice within. But it is too late, and he has no time left to contemplate changing his course of action. Spurred on by Hamlet's friendly taunt, he now moves in for the kill.

Hamlet Come for the third, Laertes. You do but dally.
I pray you pass with your best violence.
I am afeard you make a wanton[92] of me.

Laertes Say you so? Come on

They resume playing, and Laertes holds to his original intent to kill Hamlet. He has tragically failed to heed his conscience until it is too late.

Osric Nothing neither way.

Laertes Have at you now!

Laertes finally delivers the fatal wound to Hamlet. In the intense scuffling that follows, they change weapons. Now the poisoned rapier is in Hamlet's hand.

King Part them; they are incensed.

Hamlet Nay, come again.

Hamlet wounds Laertes with his own poison. Now the whole charade falls apart, and the terrible reality is revealed to all. The poisoned Queen falls.

Osric Look to the Queen there, ho!

Horatio They bleed on both sides. How is it, my lord?

Osric How is't, Laertes?

Laertes Why, as a woodcock to mine own springe,[93] Osric.
I am justly killed with mine own treachery.

Faced with the final reality of death, things become clear to Laertes. All his mundane concerns, including his obsession with reputation, now bear the unmistakable quality of irrelevance, and he openly admits his treachery.

---

92 **wanton** spoiled child

93 **springe** trap

Hamlet How does the Queen?

King She swoons to see them bleed.

The King, ever the Machiavellian schemer, tries to cover up his treachery but is gainsaid dramatically by the Queen herself.

Queen No, no, the drink, the drink! Oh my dear Hamlet!
The drink, the drink! I am poisoned.

In her dying voice, the Queen reaches out to Hamlet. She realizes too late the error of playing along with Claudius. His treachery finally hits home, and she dies with the terrible realization.

Hamlet Oh villainy! Ho! Let the door be locked.
Treachery! Seek it out.

Laertes It is here, Hamlet. Hamlet thou art slain.
No medicine in the world can do thee good;
In thee there is not half an hour of life.
The treacherous instrument is in thy hand,
Unbated and envenomed. The foul practice[94]
Hath turned itself on me. Lo, here I lie,
Never to rise again. Thy mother's poisoned.
I can no more. The King—the King's to blame.

Laertes, in his death throes, also sees everything clearly and exposes the whole charade. In this climactic duel scene, Shakespeare provides a powerful image of the inevitable outcome of hiding from the profound by artificially beautifying reality. The truth will be inexorably laid bare in the end, and tragically, because of our folly in hiding from it, we will be caught totally unprepared.

Hamlet The point envenomed too! Then, venom, to thy work.

Hamlet, realizing the treachery around him, launches himself at the King with swift fury and stabs him with the poisoned rapier.

All Treason! Treason!

King Oh yet defend me, friends. I am but hurt.

---

94 **practice** plot

The King's denial of the truth has genuinely reached pathological proportions. Even in the throes of death, he still denies his personal mortality.

Hamlet Here, thou incestuous, murd'rous, damned Dane,
Drink off this potion. Is thy union here?
Follow my mother.

With these words, Hamlet unleashes all his pent-up fury onto the King. He pours the poison into his mouth and taunts him with a pun on the word "union," here referring both to the pearl in the cup and to the King joining his mother in death. Even in his last act of vengeance, Hamlet yet spews out his loathing for the incestuous marriage between his mother and the King.

Laertes He is justly served.
It is a poison tempered[95] by himself.
Exchange forgiveness with me, noble Hamlet.
Mine and my father's death come not upon thee,
Nor thine on me.

Little remains of the Laertes who vowed revenge bitter enough to "cut his throat i'th'church." His inevitable confrontation with the profound strips away all his mundane delusions. The tragedy lies in his failure to face up to the truth earlier.

Hamlet Heaven make thee free of it. I follow thee.
I am dead, Horatio. Wretched Queen, adieu!
You that look pale and tremble at this chance,
That are but mutes or audience to this act,
Had I but time—as this fell sergeant, Death,
Is strict in his arrest—Oh, I could tell you—
But let it be. Horatio, I am dead,
Thou livest. Report me and my cause aright
To the unsatisfied.

Horatio Never believe it.
I am more an antique Roman[96] than a Dane.
Here's yet some liquor left.

---

95 **tempered** mixed

96 **antique Roman** one who prefers suicide in situations of this nature

Hamlet	As thou'rt a man Give me the cup. Let go, by heaven I'll have't. Oh God, Horatio, what a wounded name, Things standing thus unknown, shall I leave behind me. If thou didst ever hold me in thy heart, Absent thee from felicity awhile, And in this harsh world draw thy breath in pain To tell my story.

After being responsible, directly or indirectly, for the death of so many around him, Hamlet's last dying act, significantly, is to save the life of his friend. Hamlet is no longer trapped in the role of avenger, and his injunction for Horatio to clear his name and to tell his story compels Horatio to obey.

Hamlet	What warlike noise is this?
Osric	Young Fortinbras, with conquest come from Poland, To the ambassadors of England gives This warlike volley.

The sound of cannon volleys and war drums in the background intensifies the drama.

Hamlet	Oh, I die, Horatio. The potent poison quite o'ercrows[97] my spirit. I cannot live to hear the news from England, But I do prophesy th'election lights On Fortinbras. He has my dying voice. So tell him, with th'occurrents[98] more and less Which have solicited[99]—the rest is silence.

Hamlet is cut off in mid-sentence. This is the nature of death—it may come suddenly and not wait for us to complete our plans. Also, by cutting off Hamlet abruptly, Shakespeare throws us once again face to

97 **o'ercrows** overpowers

98 **occurrents** occurrences

99 **solicited** instigated

face with the ultimate mystery. This is what we must prepare to face, for the readiness is all.

Horatio Now cracks a noble heart. Good night, sweet prince,
And flights of angels sing thee to thy rest!

Horatio voices the final unforgettable eulogy for Hamlet. We are again reminded of the Hamlet who was the "expectancy and rose of the fair state" and who, indeed, would have lived up to it, had not the dreaded injunction for revenge overthrown his noble mind.

Horatio Why does the drum come hither?

Fortinbras and his soldiers arrive with the English ambassadors and are confronted with the terrible spectacle of the death of the entire Danish royalty.

Fortinbras Where is this sight?

Horatio What is it you would see?
If aught of woe or wonder, cease your search.

Fortinbras This quarry[100] cries on havoc.[101] Oh proud Death,
What feast is toward[102] in thine eternal cell,
That thou so many princes at a shot
So bloodily hast struck?

First Ambassador The sight is dismal;
And our affairs from England come too late.
The ears are senseless that should give us hearing
To tell him his commandment is fulfilled,
That Rosencrantz and Guildenstern are dead.
Where should we have our thanks?

With the confirmed demise of Rosencrantz and Guildenstern, we know that all the main characters except Horatio are now dead. This is as Shakespeare intends, to stress the inevitability of death. All the dead characters, apart from Hamlet, served to portray the entire spectrum of our futile attempts to hide from this truth. In the end, no one escapes.

---

[100] **quarry** pile of bodies

[101] **cries on havoc** proclaims a massacre

[102] **toward** in preparation

In a brilliant touch of Shakespearean irony, every one of these characters meets the inevitable as a result of exactly the method each employed to hide from its reality. The King dies as a result of his treacherous indulgence in seeking power and self-gratification, which is fuelled by his refusal to see the truth and acknowledge the folly of his actions. The Queen dies as a result of obstinately standing by Claudius—even after being informed of his evil nature—in her quest for refuge in material security and physical comforts. Polonius dies as a result of his indulgence in pseudo-intellectual pursuits and petty court intrigues, used as a means to hide from the profound. Ophelia dies from the insanity caused by the dissolution of the false security she derived from conforming to the mores of society. Laertes dies as a result of his own devious revenge plot aimed at securing his reputation and family name. Finally, Rosencrantz and Guildenstern die in the course of their blind pursuit of advancement in their worldly careers. Thus, all of them meet their end as a result of exactly the futile method each employed to hide from the reality of death.

Now Horatio begins to unravel the web of deceit surrounding the tragedy, exposing the horrific chain of events that stem from the failure of those involved to be true to themselves.

Horatio Not from his mouth,
Had it th'ability of life to thank you.
He never gave commandment for their death.
But since, so jump [103] upon this bloody question,
You from the Polack wars, and you from England,
Are here arrived, give order that these bodies
High on a stage be placed to the view,
And let me speak to the yet unknowing world
How these things came about. So shall you hear
Of carnal, bloody, and unnatural acts,
Of accidental judgments, casual [104] slaughters,
Of deaths put on by cunning and forced cause,
And, in this upshot, purposes mistook
Fallen on th'inventors' heads. All this can I
Truly deliver.

---

103 **jump** precisely

104 **casual** unplanned, chance

Horatio's message, ostensibly meant for those now at the Danish court, is also Shakespeare's way of addressing his audience. For the unnatural acts, accidental judgments, and mistaken purposes are what we have to avoid by facing the truth instead of preoccupying ourselves with distractions in a futile attempt to hide from it.

Fortinbras Let us haste to hear it,
And call the noblest to the audience.
For me, with sorrow I embrace my fortune.
I have some rights of memory[105] in this kingdom,
Which now to claim my vantage doth invite me.

Of all three—Hamlet, Laertes, and Fortinbras—who have cause to avenge their fathers, it is the one who gave up on vengeance who finally ascends the throne of Denmark.

Horatio Of that I shall have also cause to speak,
And from his mouth whose voice will draw on[106] more.
But let this same be presently performed
Even while men's minds are wild, lest more mischance
On plots and errors happen.

Horatio also voices Shakespeare's last words to the audience. We have essentially witnessed the consequences of men's wild minds—minds filled with delusions caused by denying the truth and falsely beautifying reality. It is the delusions that are the source of our problems, and among the worst of them is the delusion of vengeance.

Significantly, the ghost does not return; he has no role left to play. It is left to Fortinbras, the one who rescinded his own calling for vengeance, to voice what might have been for Hamlet:

Fortinbras Let four captains
Bear Hamlet like a soldier to the stage,
For he was likely, had he been put on,
To have proved most royal; and for his passage,
The soldier's music and the rite of war
Speak loudly for him.

---

[105] **rights of memory** traditional rights

[106] **draw on** influence

Take up the bodies. Such a sight as this
Becomes the field,[107] but here shows much amiss.
Go, bid the soldiers shoot.

Hamlet was a courageous and sensitive soul who directly faced the profound and had great potential for spiritual attainment. The call to vengeance, however, destroyed him. Perhaps Hamlet might not have made king, but his potential for attaining what is truly important, in light of the profound mystery we all face, should never have been denied him. Herein lies the true tragedy of Hamlet.

---

[107] **field** battlefield

Epilogue: The Spiritual Path

Hamlet is nothing less than an artistic miracle. From the opening scene's evocation of man's mystery world to the brilliant finale of a mortal duel disguised behind a veil of hypocrisy, Shakespeare meticulously crafts a deep and profound message for mankind. Although we may not explicitly recognize this message, just as Hamlet failed to recognize the inner voice that causes him to delay his vengeance, the play has, for centuries, gripped us in a strange and profound way, touching the inner depths of many with its poetic and haunting images. *Hamlet* has this enthralling mystical quality because it echoes something deep within us.

Yet it is important that we also recognize the message clearly, for it is the same message that sages and mystics of the past have long tried to impress on suffering humanity. Shakespeare delivers the message in a most unique way, by reaching us through our emotional involvement and getting us to directly experience the truth of it. *Hamlet* is thus akin to a mystery play enacted as a form of initiation, an experiential introduction to the inner secrets that lie within our own depths.

The play is a carefully crafted symphonic tapestry with related interweaving themes recurring throughout. To appreciate fully the beauty of the structure and the interplay of the elements, we must recognize clearly the following themes of the play:

- The need to recognize the mystery world we are all in and the importance of accepting the inevitability of death and facing the profound.
- Our propensity, instead, to hide from the truth by indulging in distractions, and by artificially beautifying what is rotten inside.
- How, as a result of being false to ourselves in this way, we become false to others.
- The question we need to ask of whether we are not, in fact, mad in doing all this.

- Why revenge and condemnation of others is wrong, and how an acceptance of reality and the inevitability of death, coupled with this frame of mind, is a disaster.

There can be no doubt that these are the main themes in the play because they reverberate through it like an endless echo. The thematic resonance and the focused allegorical scenes portraying these themes form an unmistakable cohesive unity. The mastery of Shakespeare lies in his artistry in weaving them all into a unified drama of haunting poetic brilliance. It is a play with a deep message that essentially points to an exhortation for us to face the profound and to take the spiritual path. But what exactly does "taking the spiritual path" mean?

The answer is as disarmingly simple as it is difficult to implement. It is essentially the message of the Buddha in a scripture known as the *Kalama Sutta*. This message is a universal one and applies to people of all religions and even to those who do not profess any religion.

In the *Kalama Sutta*, the Kalamas, who are the inhabitants of Kesaputta, ask the Buddha for guidance regarding a problem that is still prevalent today. This is what they say to the Buddha: [1]

> 'There are some monks and brahmins, venerable sir, who visit Kesaputta. They expound and explain only their own doctrines, the doctrines of others they despise, revile, and pull to pieces. Some other monks and brahmins too, venerable sir, come to Kesaputta. They also expound and explain only their own doctrines; the doctrines of others they despise, revile, and pull to pieces. Venerable sir, there is doubt, there is uncertainty in us concerning them, "Which of these reverend monks and brahmins spoke the truth and which falsehood?"'

The reply of the Buddha would probably astonish those who think that all religions are based on blind faith. This is what the Buddha advises the Kalamas:

> 'It is proper for you, Kalamas, to doubt, to be uncertain; uncertainty has arisen in you about what is doubtful. Come,

1 Excerpts are from the *Anguttara Nikaya*, Sutta No. 65.

> Kalamas. Do not go upon what has been acquired by repeated hearing; nor upon tradition; nor upon rumor; nor upon what is in a scripture; nor upon surmise; nor upon an axiom; nor upon specious reasoning; nor upon a bias towards a notion that has been pondered over; nor upon another's seeming ability; nor upon the consideration, "The monk is our teacher."
>
> Kalamas, when you yourselves know: "These things are bad; these things are blamable; these things are censured by the wise; undertaken and observed, these things lead to harm and ill," abandon them.
>
> Kalamas, when you yourselves know: "These things are good; these things are not blamable; these things are praised by the wise; undertaken and observed, these things lead to benefit and happiness," enter on and abide in them.'

Essentially, the Buddha is asking us to be walking question marks. The real key in the message, however, lies in the last part of the Buddha's statement, and in the word "know." When we know within ourselves that something is bad for us, and that each of us would be a better person without it, we are to act on this inner knowledge and abandon what we know to be bad. Likewise, when we know within ourselves that something is good for us, that each of us would be a better person with it, we are to act on this inner knowledge, and adopt what we know to be good. The key, then, is to act on what we each *know* is required to transform into a better person.

Every one of us knows at least one thing we can do to transform into a better person. This then is the next step we have to take. We must act on it. We have to take every next step that we each *know* is required to transform into a better person. When we have achieved that step immediately before us, we will always know the next step following that. The process is akin to climbing a mountain—the view gets clearer with each new height we reach. And if we continue this process, we will reach the very summit. Unfortunately, if we refuse the next step before us, that is where we stop.

We have to cross every threshold we know we have to cross, for there is no other way to progress.

The spiritual path is a path of aspiration, of determination to always take the next step before us. It requires total commitment, and thus the need for us to perceive the inevitability of death and the truth of our situation. For this will empower us with the will to overcome all challenges hurled at us. This is why Shakespeare stresses in *Hamlet* the need for us to accept our mortality and to face the profound.

While the spiritual path is a long, arduous journey, it is also one of profound joy and deep compassion to save each and every being from suffering. Thus, revenge as well as the condemnation of others has no place in it, and this is why Shakespeare portrays in *Hamlet* the grievous error of pursuing a path of vengeance. What is required, instead, is the process of *metanoia*,[2] the total transformation of our being to one who loves our neighbor as ourselves, the process Jesus repeatedly exhorts us to undertake.

In addition to the two main themes in the play—the need to face the truth and the error of revenge and condemnation—Shakespeare further elaborates on the nature of the spiritual path in the four scenes of Act III.

In Scene 1, Hamlet's soliloquy presents the suffering nature of our mundane existence, and his dialogue with Ophelia presents the sinful nature of man. The first serves as another powerful motivation for us to embark on the route to salvation, while the second essentially tells us what needs to be done.

Scene 2 focuses on the need for sustained effort at any quest of transformation, and this particularly applies to the spiritual quest. We cannot hope to succeed merely through intermittent commitment at times of passion. On the spiritual quest, we need to transform ourselves into one who focuses purely on higher aspirations without distractions from mundane cravings.

Scene 3 stresses the need for us to act on our convictions and aspirations. The King's failure in prayer demonstrates the inadequacy of merely repenting without transforming ourselves to fit our aspirations. The spiritual path requires *metanoia*—not the mere expression of regret—because it is the transformation of our mind towards the spiritual ideal that allows us to directly experience the higher spiritual truths.

---

2 For further explanation of *metanoia*, see pp. 99-100.

In Scene 4, the words of Hamlet present the basic requirement at each step in transforming our being:

> Assume a virtue if you have it not.
> That monster, custom, who all sense doth eat
> Of habits devil,[3] is angel yet in this,
> That to the use[4] of actions fair and good
> He likewise gives a frock or livery
> That aptly is put on. Refrain tonight,
> And that shall lend a kind of easiness
> To the next abstinence, the next more easy;
> For use almost can change the stamp of nature,
> And either the devil or throw him out
> With wondrous potency.

Spiritual practice is essentially a practice of simulating the behavior of a spiritually advanced being. If we persist long enough, our mind will take on this nature, and ultimately that is what we will become, naturally and spontaneously. The truth is already within us. It is our master within, our Buddha nature, the kingdom of heaven within us. With the transformation of our outer nature to one that will accommodate this truth, our inner light will burst forth spontaneously.

The nature of this process also means that the spiritual path is a path of verification. We are guided to know each next step that is required; it is a route of an ever-deepening realization of the truth that is already within us. All of us have the means to verify this for ourselves simply by embarking on the path of transforming ourselves to each higher ideal that we can perceive. As we reach higher and higher levels, we enter into different states of being and ultimately into spiritual bliss and universal compassion, a state of nonseparation and a deep realization of the oneness of all.

The spiritual path is not dependent on blind faith or on what we choose to believe. It is a process of gnosis that can be verified. However, the only way to verify is to experience it directly. We have to take the spiritual path ourselves. We must realize that there is nothing more crucial in our lives, for all else pales to irrelevance.

---

3 **of habits devil** acts like a devil in maintaining bad habits

4 **use** practice

This truth is reflected in the plays of Shakespeare, who is not only an extraordinary poet but a mystic of the highest order. His plays are not written merely for entertainment or merely for the sake of art. Every one of them is meticulously crafted to help initiate us into the higher spiritual principles. Each play delivers a message touching on different aspects of the spiritual path. It is important, for the sake of humanity, that we recognize these messages. For a realization of their meaning transforms the plays from mere entertainment and art into powerful experiences of the spiritual truths of the universe.

About the Author

Kenneth K. C. Chan was born in Malaysia and currently lives in Singapore. He holds university degrees in both medicine and physics, and has formerly worked as a doctor in Singapore and as a scientific editor for World Scientific. He is a follower of Tibetan Buddhism and a student of Western Mysticism, with a deep interest in the interactions between the spiritual traditions and the arts and sciences.

He wrote an original scientific paper on the theory of relativity entitled *Time and Space,* which was approved for publication by Kip Thorne, the Physics Nobel Laureate in 2017. The paper explains for the first time why the speed of light is constant (based on his understanding of both relativity and human physiology) and was published in 1993 in the ISPE anthology: *Thinking on the Edge.*

In 2004, he published the first edition of *Quintessence of Dust: The Mystical Meaning of Hamlet.* The book was nominated for the Book of the Year award by Foreword Magazine in 2004.

In 2016, he wrote an online article, *Why Relativity Exists,* which presents the key findings of his paper, *Time and Space,* to a general audience. It emphasizes that consciousness is a critical component of our reality. In the same year, he also wrote another online paper entitled *A Direct Experiential Interpretation of Quantum Mechanics*, which shows how the Buddhist Madhyamika philosophy solves the mystery of quantum physics.

In 2021, he published an online article entitled *The Spiritual Path*, which shows the remarkable synchronicity between Madhyamika philosophy, the Noble Eightfold Path, the Kabbalah Tree of Life, and the Tarot. This synchronicity reveals that the different spiritual traditions draw their inspiration from the same source, and together provides us with a map depicting the stages of the spiritual quest on the path to enlightenment.

The above online articles can be viewed at the author's website at kenneth-chan.com.